Illicit Trade

Strengthening Governance and Reducing Corruption Risks to Tackle Illegal Wildlife Trade

LESSONS FROM EAST AND SOUTHERN AFRICA

Please cite this publication as:
OECD (2018), *Strengthening Governance and Reducing Corruption Risks to Tackle Illegal Wildlife Trade: Lessons from East and Southern Africa*, Illicit Trade, OECD Publishing, Paris.
https://doi.org/10.1787/9789264306509-en

ISBN 978-92-64-30649-3 (print)
ISBN 978-92-64-30650-9 (pdf)

Series: Illicit Trade
ISSN 2617-5827 (print)
ISSN 2617-5835 (online)

Photo credits: Cover Illustration © Jeffrey Fisher

Corrigenda to OECD publications may be found on line at: *www.oecd.org/publishing/corrigenda*.

Foreword

Governance frameworks are fundamental for enabling economic integration and securing free trade. While free trade contributes to prosperity and helps lift millions out of poverty, globalisation also creates vulnerabilities that can be exploited by criminal networks at the expense of public safety, human rights and environmental resources. Such vulnerabilities enable, among other forms of trafficking, the global scourge that is the illegal wildlife trade, which erodes natural resources and undermines the long-term viability of ecosystems and diversity. The consequences of this trade are thus particularly dire for poorer rural communities in source and transit countries.

The aim of the study was to map and better understand vulnerabilities caused by illicit trade and to explore ways to tackle it effectively through enforcement and governance frameworks. The study was conducted in the Public Governance Directorate by the Secretariat of the OECD Task Force on Countering Illicit Trade (TF-CIT), under the auspices of the OECD High Level Risk Forum (HLRF). The study benefitted from over 100 field interviews in Kenya, Tanzania, Uganda and Zambia, as well as findings generated from global seizure data from WCO and TRAFFIC databases complemented by desk-based research.

This study focuses on the case of illegal wildlife trade in select countries in East and Southern Africa. The perception of this crime as being “low-risk, high-reward” has made it particularly attractive to criminal networks. These networks are able to pay public officials and other actors along the supply chain to turn a blind eye, provide inside information or otherwise abuse their position of public authority to enable such trade. The range of institutions and governments officials who are targeted and at risk underscores the need for urgent action.

This report looks at institutional capacities to counter illegal wildlife trade, and the gaps in public accountability that enable criminals to circumvent the law. The findings contribute to a more structured understanding of the gaps in governance frameworks that enable corruption and keep the illegal wildlife supply chain moving. The report offers a number of recommendations to government bodies interested in addressing this nefarious form of illicit trade, including donor agencies and law enforcement bodies, but also international organisations and NGOs engaged in the fight against illegal wildlife trade.

Acknowledgements

The report was prepared by the OECD Public Governance Directorate, led by Marcos Bonturi.

The report was written under the supervision of Stéphane Jacobzone, Deputy Head of Division, Reform of the Public Sector, and Jack Radisch, Senior Project Manager. It was drafted by Michael Morantz, Policy Analyst. Polen Cisneros provided research support and quantitative analysis. The questionnaires benefitted from internal review and comments from Julio Bacio Terracino and other experts in the Public Sector Integrity Division headed by Janos Bertok.

The fieldwork was co-ordinated thanks to Ms. Elizabeth Gitari. The authors wish to acknowledge the help received from the Royal United Services Institute for Defence and Security Studies. The authors would like to express their sincere gratitude for the seizure data provided by the World Customs Organisation (WCO) and for an open source dataset received from the wildlife organisation TRAFFIC. The authors are also grateful to the Investigation and Evidence team at World Animal Protection.

The authors express their gratitude for the numerous invaluable comments from the members of the OECD Task Force on Countering Illicit Trade who provided expertise and guidance throughout this project. In addition, the authors would like to acknowledge the 102 individuals (who shall remain anonymous) across Kenya, Tanzania, Uganda and Zambia, who provided insights and information in their capacity as enforcement officers, senior civil servants, magistrates, prosecutors, academics, international experts, NGO directors, field officers and others. The authors are grateful to these dedicated individuals who have volunteered their time and efforts to contributing their first-hand experiences, research, analyses and information to making this report as detailed and accurate as possible.

In addition, the authors would like to thank the different expert reviewers who contributed their time and expertise to ensure the rigour and quality of this report. In particular, the authors wish to thank Tim Steele and Javier Montaño (UNODC); Rob Parry Jones (WWF); Steven Broad and Sabri Zain (TRAFFIC); and Mark Shaw (Global Initiative against Transnational Organized Crime).

The authors are grateful to Liv Gaunt and Andrea Uhrhammer for their editorial and production support.

The authors would like to dedicate this book to the memory of Mr. Esmond Bradley Martin (1941-2018) and Mr. Wayne Lotter (1965-2017), whose lifetime achievements and research have helped to advance the protection of species and ecosystems across East and Southern Africa and around the world.

Table of contents

Tables

Figures

Boxes

Acronyms and Abbreviations

ACC	Anti-Corruption Commission of Zambia
CITES	Convention on International Trade in Endangered Species
DNPW	Department for National Protection of Wildlife of Zambia
EACC	Ethics and Anti-Corruption Commission of Kenya
HLRF	High Level Risk Forum
IG	Inspectorate of Government of Uganda
IWT	Illegal Wildlife Trade
KWS	Kenya Wildlife Service
NCAA	Ngorongoro Conservation Area Authority
NTAP	National Taskforce for Anti-Poaching of Tanzania
ODPP	Office of the Director of Public Prosecutions of Kenya
PCCB	Prevention and Combating of Corruption Bureau of Tanzania
PIKE	Proportion of Illegally Killed Elephants
SDG	Sustainable Development Goals
SWIFT	Special Wildlife Integrated Force for Tourism of Uganda
TANAPA	Tanzania National Parks Authority
TAWA	Tanzania Wildlife Management Authority
TF-CIT	Task Force on Countering Illicit Trade
UNCAC	United Nations Convention Against Corruption
UNODC	United Nations Office for Drugs and Crime
UWA	Uganda Wildlife Authority
WCMA	Wildlife Conservation and Management of Kenya
WCO	World Customs Organisation
WWF	World Wildlife Fund
ZAWA	Zambia Wildlife Authority

Executive Summary

Like all forms of illicit trade, the illegal wildlife trade (IWT) causes physical, societal, economic, and environmental harm. At the source, IWT affects communities, undermining economies and undercutting livelihoods that rely upon sustainable resource use.

Governance gaps facilitate IWT. Criminals reduce their exposure to risk by bribing their way out of arrests, investigations, prosecution and convictions. It is commonly acknowledged that IWT could not take place on a global scale without corruption. Yet efforts to address this key enabler of IWT fall far short, revealing wider governance and institutional challenges that undermine effective law enforcement and perpetuate the status of IWT as a low-risk and high-reward crime.

This study, based on information from practitioners and experts on the front lines of combatting IWT, finds that these governance gaps and risks of corruption are far more complex and diverse than was previously thought. Global seizure records from the World Customs Organisation and the wildlife organisation TRAFFIC show that IWT takes place on roads, in maritime ports and airports. While arrests for trafficking in wildlife have increased in recent years, most of the time no action is taken against the corrupt persons who facilitate these transactions in source and transit countries enabling the illegal export of wildlife to consumer markets, including OECD countries. In the focus countries of this study, not one single criminal prosecution for IWT was identified that led to corruption charges, let alone convictions.

A series of high-level statements in fora such as CITES and more recently the G20 recognise the need to address corruption as part of intensive international efforts to counter IWT. However, only a handful of donors and NGOs have integrated targeted anti-corruption initiatives into their development and conservation programmes. Instead, focus remains firmly on the predicate offences of poaching and trafficking. Yet, without explicitly targeting the corrupt enablers of IWT, efforts focused on criminal actors will have a limited effect.

In order to tackle the governance gaps and the risk of corruption at the right level, governments and the international community should enact a fundamental change in approach to IWT, explicitly targeting the corrupt officials and structures that facilitate this lucrative form of transnational crime.

Key findings

- Corruption is a critical enabler of the illegal wildlife trade (IWT). Its forms are diverse and dynamic, evolving in line with specific institutional and supply-chain factors.
- Corruption takes place at sourcing, transit and export stages, and involves public and private sector abuses of power and trust. At sourcing level, it can be *ad hoc*, involving smaller sums of money and lower-level officials. At stages of

consolidation, international transit and export, it is often systemic, involves larger sums of money, higher-level officers, and is generally pre-planned.

- The profile of corruption risks linked to IWT varies: in any given area some, none or all of the risks identified in this study may be present, at any given time.
- Where seizures take place, authorities often do not investigate the corrupt officials who enabled the supply stream at earlier points in the trafficking chain.
- In the few reported cases where officials have been arrested in possession of illegal wildlife products, they are charged with poaching or trafficking. but not investigated for corruption.
- Anti-corruption authorities rarely prioritise corruption linked to IWT, and wildlife management authorities typically address corruption within their ranks as a disciplinary issue rather than a criminal offence.
- Anti-corruption is not a focus area for NGOs concerned with IWT. Yet, anti-corruption – and particularly preventative work – is crucial where trafficking can hasten the disappearance of species.
- There is no comprehensive quantitative data on corruption linked to IWT in the focus countries.

Summary of recommendations

For government agencies

- Liaise with financial intelligence units and anti-corruption agencies in the pursuit of parallel financial and anti-corruption investigations in all IWT cases.
- Develop and implement standard operating procedures for IWT prosecutions, adopt case management procedures and sentencing guidelines.
- Review witness and whistle-blower protection mechanisms. Treat all forms of corruption linked to IWT as a criminal offence, and reward integrity.
- Bolster co-operation between anti-corruption authorities and wildlife conservation actors. Informal and formal alliances such as multi-agency task forces at national and international level, can help to reduce corruption risks.
- In anti-corruption interventions, prioritise the most critical points along the trade chain and develop specific responses to corruption risks at those points.
- Prioritise systematic collection of corruption incident data to better understand the scale of the problem and its dynamics for future investigations.
- Leverage international investigative co-operation, and foster multinational operations that target the criminal networks that seek to co-opt and corrupt.
- Ensure capacity is developed to enforce obligations under international legal frameworks, such as the United Nations Convention against Corruption.
- Encourage an active role for civil society in drawing attention to suspicious activity during cases under investigation and before the courts, and in publicising relevant convictions.

For development agencies, donors and NGOs

- Build anti-corruption impact assessments into all levels of programming for future IWT interventions. Explicitly address corruption as a key component of donor-funded projects.
- Conduct capacity building through training anti-corruption authorities on issues specific to IWT and support them in the delivery of anti-corruption training for wildlife management authorities as well as assisting in developing public awareness campaigns to encourage IWT-related reporting.
- Support officer exchanges and long-term secondments between wildlife management authorities and anti-corruption agencies.
- Provide IWT-focused awareness-raising for prosecutors and magistrates.
- Support the development of an electronic permit system for trade in CITES species and the creation of a centralised database to reduce risks of physical forgery.
- Support the systematic collection of data on corruption related to IWT and promote the creation of common reporting standards.

1. Introduction: Understanding the impact of the illegal wildlife trade and the need for change

This chapter offers a background on IWT, highlighting the impact of these crimes from an international perspective. This section highlights the scale of IWT in the region and historical trends that underline the importance of conducting this study. Finally, the chapter outlines the methodology of the report.

'Corruption is an insidious plague that has a wide range of corrosive effects on societies. ... This evil phenomenon is found in all countries, big and small, rich and poor, but it is in the developing world that its effects are most destructive.' (UN, 2004[1])

There is strong recognition within the international community of the wide-reaching, pernicious impacts of corruption on development. Whether undermining rule of law, eroding quality of life, distorting markets or enabling threats to human security, the effects of corruption on economic, social and political life have been extensively documented. In response, an increasingly comprehensive range of policy and practical tools has been deployed to disrupt the perpetuation of corruption, both domestically and internationally, in a range of sectors. At the OECD, the Public Governance policy community has developed several important OECD Instruments in this area, including the 2017 OECD Council Recommendation on Public Integrity, updating an earlier instrument, and the 2003 OECD Council Recommendation on Managing Conflicts of Interest in the Public Service. These instruments provide a strategic perspective to frame a discussion on public integrity, including how to fight corruption that acts as a facilitator of illicit trade.

The focus of such anti-corruption activity, however, has not been universal. One of the least discussed dimensions of corruption is that witnessed in the wildlife sector – and particularly that enabling illegal wildlife trade (IWT). In many affected countries, the reach of anti-corruption initiatives on the ground has failed to penetrate the wildlife domain. Here, unlike in other spheres, the precise forms of corruption enabling illegal activity are rarely considered, poorly understood and commonly overlooked in government responses.

Worldwide, IWT is one of the most profitable forms of illicit trade, forming a multi-billion-dollar industry that transcends national borders. Although significant methodological issues affect such estimates, IWT has been valued at $7–23 billion annually – part of a wider environmental crime industry valued at $91–258 billion (Nellemann; et al, 2016[2]). As it has expanded, the trade has grown in sophistication, involving regular, trans-continental transfers of multi-ton consignments. Today, it is increasingly recognised as transnational organised crime – and, as such, as activity that demands extensive, strategic facilitation by corrupt entities across the chain (Wittig, 2016[3]).

Given the scope of the criminality involved, failure to act against corruption enabling IWT exacerbates the risk of extinction of species already endangered by illegal sourcing and trafficking. Beyond this, it aggravates the human impacts of IWT, harming countries' ability to achieve anti-poverty and development outcomes. This can undermine the ability to engage in the 2030 Agenda on sustainable development and can also deprive countries of valuable touristic resources, while depleting natural species which represent a global public good. Notably, corruption and the illegal trade in wildlife it enables undermine affected countries' ability to attain Sustainable Development Goals (SDGs) 15.7 and 15.c on combating poaching and trafficking of protected species. They also inhibit SDG 16, designed to 'promote peaceful and inclusive societies for sustainable development, provide access to justice for all and build effective, accountable and inclusive institutions at all levels'.

1.1. Background

This report details the findings of research conducted over 2017 specifically into corruption that facilitates IWT in four source and transit countries: Kenya, Tanzania, Uganda and Zambia. The OECD selected these countries in light of their prominent roles at the early stages of the IWT supply chain, and the known corruption issues each faces. All act as source and transit countries for a range of wildlife products, from ivory to rhino horn, pangolin scales and hippo teeth, among numerous others. In 2017, the four ranked 143rd, 103rd, 151st and 96th, respectively, of 180 countries ranked on Transparency International's Corruption Perceptions Index (Transparency International, 2018[4]).

In examining the linkages between IWT and corruption in these countries, the report builds on previous OECD work, embodied in the Task Force on Countering Illicit Trade (TF-CIT) as well as drawing on the wider OECD work on anti-corruption and integrity, including engaging through the Integrity Forum. The TF-CIT works with Member countries to better understand the complex range of threats posed by illicit trade to global economies and well-being. IWT has formed a key focus of annual TF-CIT meetings. In 2015, the OECD co-hosted a Wilton Park meeting with the United Kingdom's Foreign and Commonwealth Office dedicated to strengthening law enforcement for wildlife crime, identifying corruption, organised crime and money laundering as key components of IWT (WP/OECD, 2015[5]). Since then, the TF-CIT has held dedicated sessions covering the shifting dynamics of this lucrative illegal trade. The 2016 OECD report 'Illicit Trade: Converging Criminal Networks' presented a dedicated chapter on IWT, focusing on trafficking trends in sub-Saharan Africa, outlining key hot spots and hubs for illegal trafficking flows (OECD, 2016[6]). In 2017, the OECD held a specific session on IWT as part of the OECD-wide Integrity Forum. Most recently, the 2018 OECD report 'Governance Frameworks to Counter Illicit Trade' has highlighted the institutional gaps facing governments in efforts to penalise illicit trade, with a dedicated study of IWT and the penalties, sanctions and national strategies of governments to address it. In an overview of select economies, it found that such crimes are typically penalised through relatively light sentences, with little pursuit of charges for associated crimes, like corruption or money laundering (OECD, 2018[7]).

This report presents the findings of research undertaken mindful of the inflection point at which the global fight against IWT now stands. Today, growing attention to the threats posed by this low-risk, high-reward crime has seen increased investment and focus on the issue by governments, NGOs and international organisations. Across Africa, this has led to relative declines in rates of elephant poaching, for example: encouragingly, 2016 represented the fifth consecutive year in which rates of illegal killing declined (CITES, 2017[8]). However, these figures mask a number of trouble spots, such as those across several countries in Central Africa, where levels of poaching remain very high. At the same time, despite the continent-wide poaching decline, in 2016 the overall elephant population remains likely to have shrunk. 2016 also saw record numbers of large-scale ivory seizures – amounting to the largest volume by weight seized since the banning of commercial international trade in 1989 (CITES, 2017[8]).

Figure 1.1. Proportion of Illegally Killed Elephants (PIKE) Regional Estimates

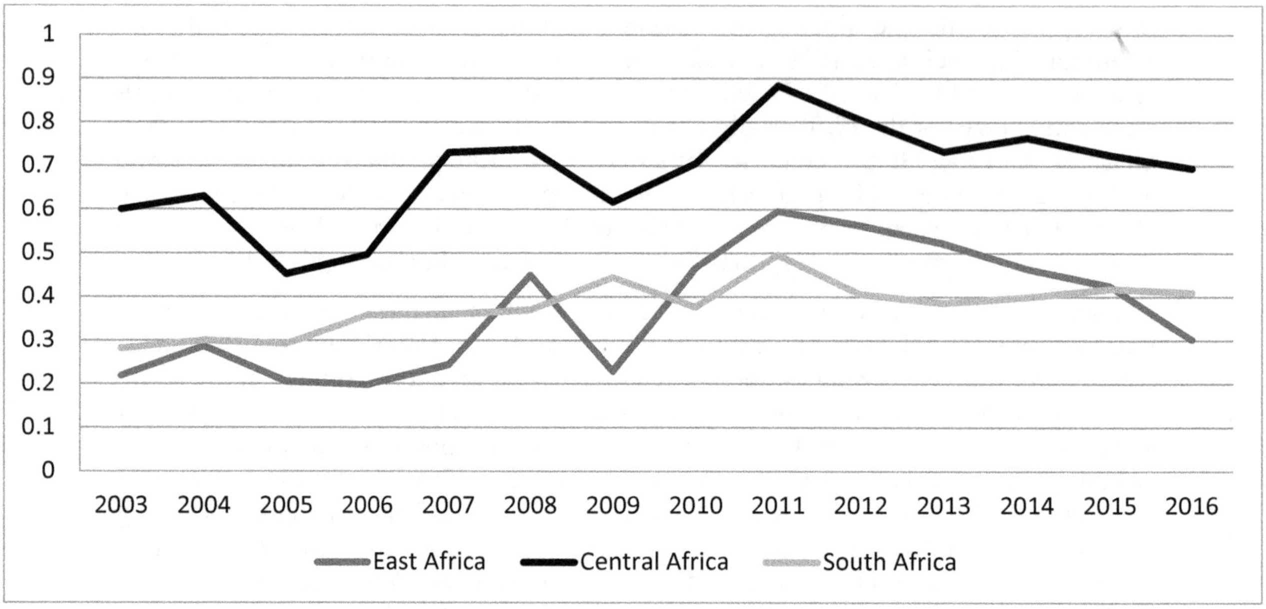

Note: According to CITES, the 'Proportion of Illegally Killed Elephants (PIKE), is calculated as the number of illegally killed elephants found divided by the total number of elephant carcasses encountered by patrols or other means, aggregated by year for each site (…) PIKE can be used to estimate numbers of elephants killed and absolute poaching rates' (CITES, 2017[9])
Source: CITES

Figure 1.2. PIKE Trends in Africa

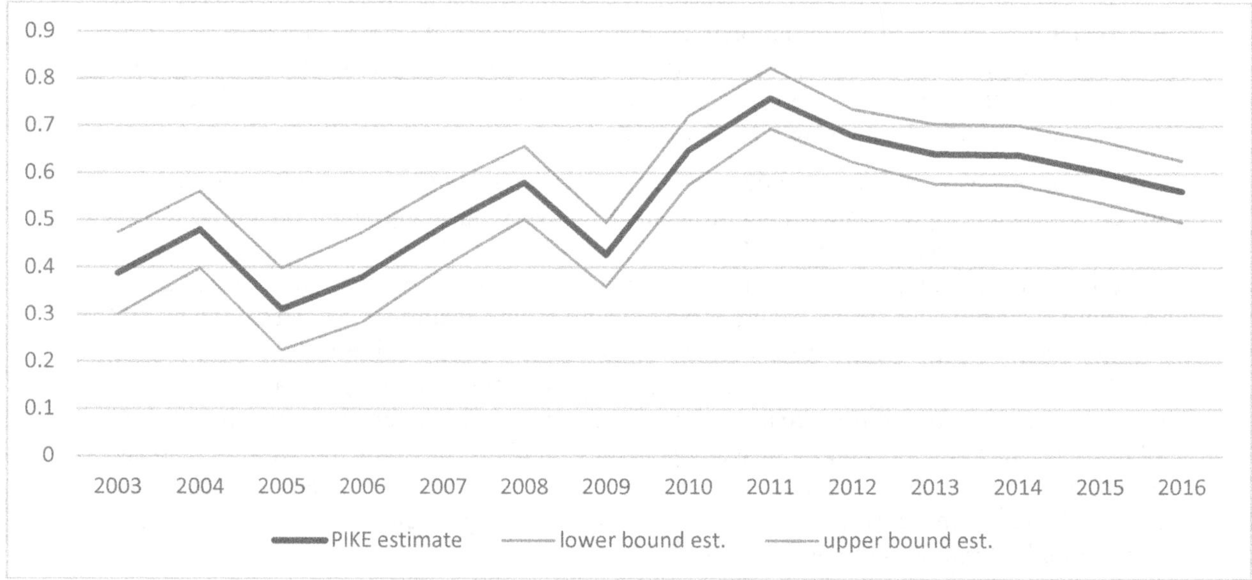

Source: CITES

Across all affected states, the failure to address the corruption enabling IWT has impeded further progress, posing a considerable risk to the ability of governments to sustainably stave off these crimes. In recognition of this threat, a number of countries and organisations have issued a series of high-level statements on the need to address corruption as an integral part of broader efforts. To give just a few examples, at the 2014 London Conference on IWT participating countries called on all states to 'adopt a zero tolerance policy on corruption associated with the illegal wildlife trade, recognising … that corruption is an important factor facilitating … the illegal wildlife trade'. The following year, the Kasane Conference reiterated the London Conference's emphasis on zero tolerance of corruption (Kasane, 2015[10]). CITES and UNODC have urged the international community to respond to 'spiralling wildlife and forest crime, fuelled by corrosive corruption' (UNODC, 2015.[11]). In 2015, UN General Assembly Resolution 69/314 called on states 'to prohibit, prevent and counter any form of corruption that facilitates illicit trafficking in wildlife' (UN, 2015[12]). The same year, the African Union's African Strategy on Combating Illegal Exploitation and Illegal Trade in Wild Fauna and Flora in Africa called for countries to "develop and/or implement programmes to prevent and combat wildlife related corruption and promoting integrity".

In 2016, meanwhile, at the 17th meeting of the Conference of the Parties, CITES issued its first-ever corruption-focused resolution, 'acknowledging the high degree of involvement of organised criminal groups … and their frequent use of corrupt practices' (CITES, 2016[13]). It did so calling on all parties 'to adopt measures to prohibit, prevent, detect and counter instances of corruption and ensure that any corrupt practices associated with the administration, regulation, implementation or enforcement of CITES are punishable as criminal offences' (CITES, 2016[13]). The same year, the Hanoi Conference on IWT 'welcome[d] and reaffirm[ed] commitments to strengthen efforts to counter corruption that facilitates the illegal trade in wildlife' (Hanoi Statement, 2016[14]). Most recently, in 2017, the G20 adopted a set of High Level Principles on Combatting Corruption Related to Illegal Trade in Wildlife and Wildlife Products. The G20 continues to focus on this issue by developing best practice in countering corruption and IWT (G20, 2017[15]). Also in 2017, the UN re-affirmed its commitment to the issue, calling on states to 'tackle illicit trafficking in wildlife, including through legislation related to money-laundering, corruption, fraud, racketeering and financial crime'. (UN, 2017[16]).

The high-level attention from multilateral fora has ensured corruption a place on the agenda across the global counter-wildlife trafficking community. However, while the issue is now an integral part of debate and discussion, it is one that few have yet felt equipped to address in practice. Indeed, those concrete interventions that exist on the ground remain relatively few and unstructured. While laudable, the aforementioned statements have not translated into comprehensive practical action or detailed donor strategies to address the issues at play. In a 2016 World Bank analysis of funding for initiatives to combat IWT, corruption-focused interventions were conspicuous in their absence[1]. Few donors or NGOs have adopted a clear anti-corruption agenda in their work, generally stopping at providing capacity building or material support to law enforcement[2].

The lack of action owes in large part to a significant lack of empirical evidence and understanding of the phenomena in question. Tellingly, little published information exists on the precise forms and dynamics of corruption that enable IWT; on the prevalence of corruption across the supply chain; or on the actors and institutions most affected (Williams et al., 2016[17]) (Smith and Walpole, 2005[18]). Preventing this has been the continued absence of investigation, prosecution, and thus reliable hard data on corruption as an enabler of IWT. Furthermore, officials have only recently begun to recognise the need to respond specifically to corruption as a key factor facilitating wildlife crime. As yet, however, in many source and transit states, not a single case of corruption linked to IWT has seen criminal proceedings under corruption charges, let alone prosecutions or convictions.

This situation has precluded the systematic recording or interrogation of corrupt activity associated with IWT. The lack of quantitative data has in turn impeded efforts to advance existing knowledge on corruption as an enabler of this crime. This state of affairs is problematic: without a clearer understanding of the form and nature of the corruption involved, governments cannot tailor their strategies to effectively target these offences. To achieve the global ambitions outlined above, there is an urgent need to expand the evidence base on the most pressing corruption risks across the IWT chain.

1.2. Purpose of the Report

The aim of this report is to enhance current understandings of the principal corruption risks around IWT in four key source and transit countries. The report focuses on Kenya, Tanzania, Uganda and Zambia and seeks to provide a structured understanding of corruption risks related to IWT within them. In doing so, the report looks to highlight key corruption risks around the mechanisms and methods corrupt actors are able to use. In doing so, it examines the structural vulnerabilities that exist within relevant institutions, and the way in which these vary along the supply chain.

The focus on corruption *risks* is important. Indeed, the dearth of substantive quantitative data and the lack of a wide baseline of convictions has limited the research conducted for this report. In this context, the report draws on alternative methods: alongside a review of relevant, existing publications and open-source media mapping exercise, it harnesses the first-hand experience of those charged with responding to IWT on the ground. Due to the anecdotal nature of their insights, the purpose of this report is to outline corruption *risks*, as opposed to quantifying confirmed instances of corrupt activity on a large scale. In presenting the findings, the report documents knowledge that is as yet largely unrecorded, but presents a key source of qualitative information on corruption risks around IWT.

This analysis is much needed. In the IWT context, policymakers, NGOs and international organisations often treat 'corruption' in monolithic terms – as a broad concept encompassing all possible risks. Governments, NGOs and researchers have made few attempts to break down the all-inclusive 'corruption' category in line with the appearance of specific risks on the ground. Such a deconstruction of corruption risks is what this report seeks to contribute – highlighting, as such, the numerous opportunities for corruption to facilitate criminal activity along the IWT chain. The comprehensive approach adopted in the report also reflects the broad reach and spirit of the OECD Recommendation on Public Integrity. The focus on institutional and governance aspects is also in line with the broader mandate of the OECD, in the public governance arena, to provide support and recommendations on governance and implementation gaps.

This report and the analysis herein will help governments to develop institutional capacities to counter both IWT and, importantly, the corruption that enables it. The findings will be useful to governments and law enforcement actors looking to conduct risk assessments, to improve management practices, and to ensure due diligence that is specifically tailored to mitigating IWT risks. Furthermore, the recommendations can assist donor countries, NGOs, and other actors – including the private sector – to better understand where targeted interventions and efforts can have the strongest impact.

The analysis and recommendations presented in this report complement existing anti-corruption and rule-of-law initiatives. Policymakers, NGOs, IOs, and the wider audience are encouraged to apply these recommendations in response to the risks present in relation to IWT. The analysis conducted herein is limited to the field of IWT, and does not cover other environmental sectors, notably logging and fisheries.[3] Finally, it is beyond the scope of the report to assess or provide recommendations to address corruption writ large across the focus countries. This is despite the clear relevance of this broader picture to the specific corruption risks identified around IWT.

For the purpose of this study, a clear definition of IWT is required. This is not a straightforward matter: the international community continues to lack a universally accepted definition and interpretations of the scope of the term vary. Some organisations use IWT to cover 'the gamut from illegal logging of protected forests to supply the demand for exotic woods, to the illegal fishing of endangered marine life for food, and the poaching of elephants to supply the demand for ivory' (US FWS, 2018[19]). Others distinguish between terrestrial species (IWT), aquatic species (illegal fishing) and timber (illegal logging).

What makes trade in wildlife and wildlife products 'illegal' is a similarly complex issue. As an international treaty, CITES provides the international legal basis for signatory parties to operate in a common manner. Yet it ultimately depends on the implementation of consistent national legislation, which varies among signatories. As such, trade in a certain species can be legal in one country and illegal under CITES – or, by contrast, prohibited under national law and permitted under CITES.

This report views illegal trade in wildlife as that which violates either international legal frameworks or the legislation of affected countries – thus encompassing both domestic law and CITES regulations. In this context, the report understands illegal trade in wildlife as the illegal taking and trade in wild species of flora and fauna, excluding illegal fishing and logging. Importantly, this understanding of the term IWT is conceived more narrowly than 'wildlife crime', excluding illegal grazing and encroachment, among other criminal activities. 'Corruption', meanwhile, is defined by Transparency International, as 'abuse of entrusted power for private gain'[4].

1.3. Methodology

The dearth of substantive quantitative data or a wide baseline of convictions poses the most significant challenge to this study. This ensures the need to develop an alternative methodology, to overcome the barriers noted above. As such, this study draws on a multi-methods approach to paint a broader picture. This comprised an extensive key word-based search of the published literature; a mapping exercise of open-source reporting on IWT and corruption; and semi-structured interview-based research in focus countries. Despite the limitations posed by the lack of quantitative data, the study represents the furthest-reaching dedicated research into corruption–IWT linkages conducted across the focus countries to date.

1.3.1. Key-word-based review of published literature

The first step of analysis involved taking stock of all relevant published literature, including public documents produced by international organisations, NGOs and governments, as well as academic papers and other relevant documents, such as briefings by domestic authorities and international declarations. A Google Scholar search on the terms ('wildlife trade' OR 'wildlife trafficking') AND 'corruption' returned 2,280 results as of 1 August 2017, of which 85 publications were analysed. As many angles as possible were sought on the issues: the review involved a core focus on both IWT and corruption to assess diverse perspectives on their intersections. The final documents were selected to achieve an optimum balance between comprehensiveness of coverage and relevance of source.

The articles were categorised according to the extent of the emphasis placed on IWT–corruption links, the strength of the evidence presented, locations and modalities examined, and publication dates. The review produced on this basis analysed the depth and breadth of existing coverage, identifying key knowledge gaps around particular locations and corruption mechanisms. The results are summarised in Chapter 2 and – with the open source media mapping – represent the baseline of existing knowledge against which the rest of the research was conducted.

1.3.2. Open source media mapping

The open source media mapping exercise was undertaken with targeted word-string searches conducted in English, French and Spanish. Searches covered the word 'ivory' AND ('poaching' OR 'seizure' OR 'trial' OR 'fraud' OR 'accused' OR 'crime' OR 'arrested' OR 'guilty' OR 'jail' OR 'suspect' OR 'bribery' OR 'laundering' OR 'corrupt')[5]. Over 300 cases were reviewed from 2008-2017, on a global scale. Information was recorded on the date and location of the alleged incident; the offence and species said to be involved; the type of corrupt actors said to be involved; the official and unofficial descriptions presented; the level of corruption said to be involved; and the current status of the case. Of the total reported cases, 17 were mapped in relation to Kenya, 19 in relation to Tanzania, 39 in relation to Uganda, and 9 in relation to Zambia.

The results of the mapping are summarised in Chapter 2, alongside the review of existing literature. It must be noted, however, that such media mapping offers a highly partial picture of corruption linked to IWT. Influenced by the limited success witnessed in investigations and prosecutions, there is an inevitable bias in media reporting towards coverage of low-level, more easily chargeable offences. At the same time, it can be assumed that reporting is more extensive in countries where journalists can operate with less fear of repercussion. As such, the mapping exercise cannot be interpreted as an accurate overview of the prevalence of or most common forms taken by corruption linked to IWT. Rather, the information is presented as an additional source of existing data – one that demands critical analysis alongside other sources.

1.3.3. Semi-Structured Interviews

From September to December 2017, 90 semi-structured interviews were carried out by the research team. Interviews were undertaken with front-line practitioners and experts active in Kenya, Tanzania, Uganda and Zambia, both face to face (93%) and by phone (7%) where based most remotely. Interviews engaged government officials (39%), NGO and independent conservation, anti-poaching and -trafficking practitioners (42%), experts based in foreign delegations (13%), and experts within international organizations, research institutes and the private sector (6%). Government agencies interviewed included:

- Wildlife management and anti-poaching authorities
- Wildlife and tourism Ministries
- Anti-corruption authorities
- Offices for public prosecutors / state attorneys
- Financial intelligence units
- Military representatives

Interviews were conducted on a semi-structured basis, using guides designed to target the knowledge gaps identified in the earlier phases of research. All interviews were carried out confidentially, and are referenced in this report through anonymised indicators. Whether trusted law-enforcement practitioners or conservationists, such frontline actors offered key insights into the everyday workings of the counter-wildlife trafficking system and its vulnerabilities to corruption, even where this goes unrecorded.

In analysing responses, researchers cross-checked findings against each other, the existing publicly available literature and the results of the open-source media mapping. The results informed the analysis presented, with information from all sources assessed to draw out commonalities and differences. Throughout, the analytical approach taken was both inductive and deductive. In the former case, researchers sought to draw outward from individual instances of corruption to identify broader patterns. In the latter case, researchers looked to reason inward to the specifics from postulates about the nature of organised criminality in each location.

Table 1.1. Reported Corruption Risks Along the Trade Chain by Institutional Actor

Below is a list of identified corruption risks that have been described and corroborated throughout semi-structured interviews. The corruption risks are identified as the activity that would be undertaken for personal gain, or for a bribe received from the criminal actors whose objective is to conduct IWT

Institutional Actor	Wildlife Ranger	Wildlife Conservation Official	Police Officer	Military	Airport Security	Customs	Investigator	Prosecutors	Magistrates	Elected officials
Poaching for possession or sale	X		X	X						X
Providing information to poachers	X	X								
Providing equipment to poachers	X	X	X							
Theft (from stocks or seizures)	X	X	X							
Direct Assistance to traffickers exchange for bribes	X		X	X	X	X				X
Granting fraudulent CITES permits		X								
Granting of hunting licenses under false pretences		X								X
Granting of permits under false pretences		X								X
Releasing persons under arrest	X	X	X							
Improper keeping of the chain of custody			X			X	X			
Granting bail pending trial despite flight risk									X	
Loss of court documents and evidence	X		X			X	X	X		
Intentional errors or mistakes in testimony or court proceedings							X	X	X	
Exclusion of admissible evidence									X	
Granting light sentences or fines									X	

Source: OECD Research

In some cases, the report omits specific detailed information to protect respondents and avoid compromising ongoing investigations. However, the report draws out the broader trends and the specific implications of these responses. Where possible, footnotes linking to media and secondary sources support the information obtained from interviews. The OECD has relied upon a select group of respondents and experts to review the methodology and findings in an effort to ensure that lessons from anonymised cases remain reflected in this report.

Figure 1.3. Breakdown of Interviews Conducted

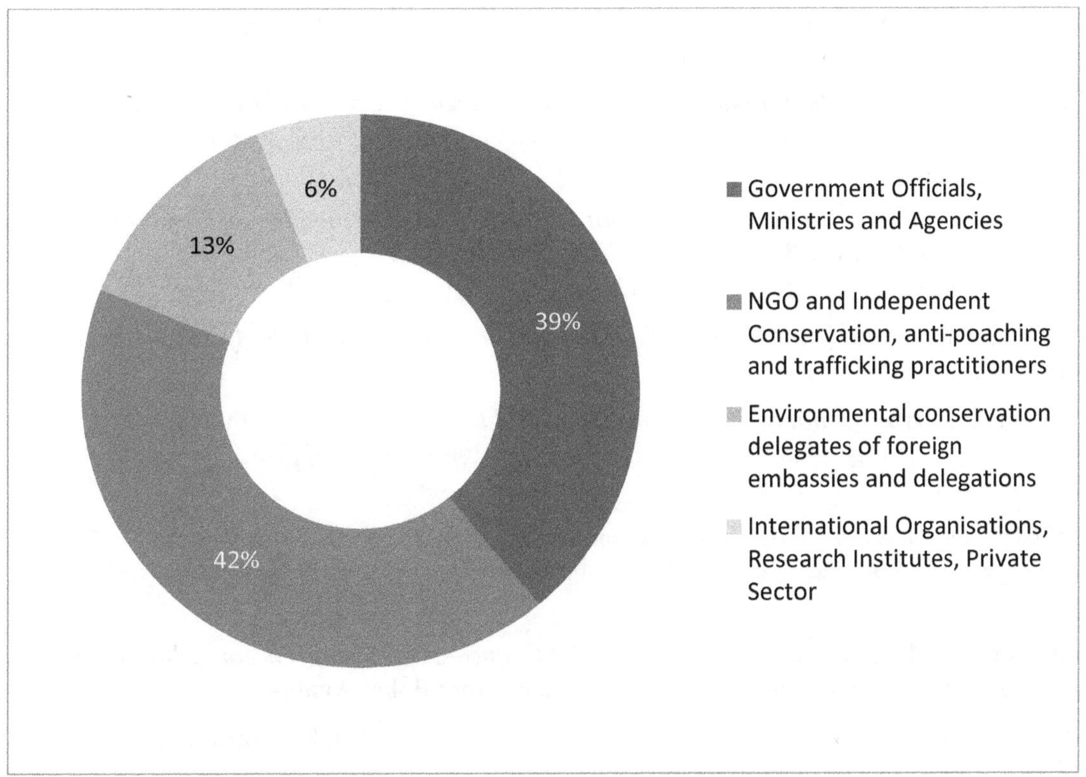

1.4. Structure of the Report

Following this Introductory chapter, the report is structured as follows:

- Chapter 2 summarises the findings of the key-word based review of literature and open-source media mapping, highlighting knowledge gaps around IWT and corruption risks.
- Chapter 3 presents insights from semi-structured interviews into the ways in which structural arrangements in place in focus countries influence corruption risks.
- Chapter 4 presents insights from semi-structured interviews into the ways in which corruption risks vary by stage of the supply chain.
- Chapter 5 presents proposals made during interviews on the most effective ways to mitigate both sets of risks.
- In the conclusion, the report presents a series of recommendations directed at domestic and external actors to address the corruption risks identified.

References

CITES (2016), *Prohibiting, Preventing and Countering Corruption Facilitating Activities Conducted in Violation of the Convention', 17th Meeting of the Conference of the Parties, Johannesburg (South Africa)*.

CITES (2017), "Status of Elephant Populations, Levels of Illegal Killing and the Trade in Ivory: A Report to the CITES Standing Committee", Vol. SC69 Doc. 51.1 Annex, p. p. 3, https://cites.org/sites/default/files/eng/com/sc/69/E-SC69-51-01-A.pdf.

CITES (2017), *African Elephant Poaching Down, Ivory Seizures Up and Hit Record High*, https://cites.org/eng/news/pr/African_elephant_poaching_down_ivory_seizures_up_and_hit_record_high_24102017.

G20 (2017), *Annex to G20 Leaders Declaration: G20 High Level Principles on Combatting Corruption Related to Illegal Trade in Wildlife and Wildlife Products*, https://www.consilium.europa.eu/media/23552/2017-g20-acwg-wildlife-en.pdf.

Haenlein, C. and M. Smith (eds.) (2016), *Wildlife Trafficking and Ecurity in Africa: Myths and Realities*, Taylor and Francis.

Hanoi Statement (2016), *Hanoi Statement on Illegal Wildlife Trade*, http://iwthanoi.vn/wp-content/themes/cites/template/statement/Hanoi%20Statement%20on%20Illegal%20Wildlife%20Trade.pdf.

Kasane (2015), *Statement from the Kasane Conference on the Illegal Wildlife Trade*, https://www.gov.uk/government/uploads/system/uploads/attachment_data/file/417231/kasane-statement-150325.pdf.

Nellemann; et al (2016), *The Rise of Environmental Crime – A Growing Threat to Natural Resources, Peace, Development and Security*, Norwegian Center for Global Analyses.

OECD (2018), *Governance Frameworks to Counter Illicit Trade*, OECD Publishing, Paris, http://dx.doi.org/10.1787/9789264291652-en.

OECD (2018), *Illicit Financial Flows: The Economy of Illicit Trade in West Africa*, OECD Publishing, http://dx.doi.org/10.1787/9789264268418-en.

OECD (2016), "Illicit Trade: Converging Criminal Networks", *OECD Reviews of Risk Management Policies*, http://dx.doi.org/10.1787/9789264251847-en..

OECD (2013), *Evading the Net: Tax Crime in the Fisheries Sector*, OECD Publishing, http://www.oecd.org/ctp/evading-the-net-tax-crime-in-the-fisheries-sector.htm.

Smith, R. and M. Walpole (2005), "Should Conservationists Pay More Attention to Corruption?", *Oryx* , Vol. 39/3.

Transparency International (2018), *Corruption Perceptions Index 2017*, https://www.transparency.org/news/feature/corruption_perceptions_index_2017.

Transparency International (2017), "Corruption Perceptions Index 2017", https://www.transparency.org/news/feature/corruption_perceptions_index_2017.

Transparency International (2003), *Annual Report 2003: What is Corruption?*, https://www.transparency.org/what-is-corruption, accessed 10 February 2018.

UN (2017), *Global Compact: Principle Ten*, https://www.unglobalcompact.org/what-is-gc/mission/principles/principle-10.

UN (2004), "UN Global Compact Principle Ten: Anticorruption", https://www.unglobalcompact.org/what-is-gc/mission/principles/principle-10.

UNEP (2018), *Framework Principles on Human Rights and the Environment*, http://rwi.lu.se/app/uploads/2018/02/knoxer.pdf.

U4 (ed.) (2016), *The Resource Bites Back: Entry-Points for Addressing Corruption in Wildlife Crime'.*

UN (2004), *United Nations Convention against Corruption (UNODC) 'Foreword', p. iii..*

UN (2015), *UN General Assembly 'Resolution Adopted by the General Assembly on 30 July 2015'.*

UN (2017), *Resolution 71/326 adopted by the General Assembly Tackling illicit trafficking in wildlife*, http://www.un.org/en/ga/search/view_doc.asp?symbol=A/RES/71/326.

UNODC (2015.), *Joint Statement of UNODC Executive Director Yury Fedotov and the Secretary-General of CITES John Scanlon on Corruption as an Enabler of Wildlife and Forest Crime.*

World Bank (2016), *Analysis of International Funding to Tackle Illegal Wildlife Trade*, http://documents.worldbank.org/curated/en/695451479221164739/pdf/110267-WP-Illegal-Wildlife-Trade-OUO-9.pdf.

WP/OECD (2015), *Wildlife crime and international security: Strengthening Law Enforcement (Monday 26 – Wednesday 28 October 2015)*, https://www.wiltonpark.org.uk/wp-content/uploads/WP1423-Report.pdf.

Notes

[1] Notably, anti-corruption initiatives did not feature in the breakdown of 'IWT intervention categories' identified by the report, despite corruption being mentioned explicitly as a key driver. See World Bank, 'Analysis of International Funding to Tackle Illegal Wildlife Trade' pp, 18–19 (World Bank, 2016[173])

[2] Although notable exceptions include the work of the Eco-Activists for Governance and Law Enforcement (EAGLE), TRAFFIC, and UNODC's Global Programme for Combating Wildlife and Forest Crime.

[3]Other work is ongoing in these areas. For example, the OECD's work on tax evasion and illegal trade in the fisheries sector describes corruption as an important driver in illegal, unlicensed and unregulated fishing (OECD, 2013[4]). A number of in-depth and regional studies have been formulated by international organisations such as Interpol and NGOs such as TRAFFIC to combat corruption related to forestry crime, both globally and on a regional basis in East Africa (INTERPOL, 2016[5]) (TRAFFIC, 2007[6]).

[4] See Transparency International, Annual Report 2003 (Transparency International, 2003[174]) This definition has come to be widely accepted among policymakers and academics: see, for example, UN Global Compact, 'Principle Ten' (UN, 2017[175])

[5] The word-string search in French was as follows: 'ivoire' AND ('braconnage' OR 'saisie' OR 'procès' OR 'fraude' OR 'accusé' OR 'crime' OR 'arrestation' OR 'culpabilité' OR 'emprisonnement' OR 'suspect' OR 'corruption' OR 'blanchiment' OR 'corruption'). The word-string search in Spanish was as follows: 'marfil' AND ('demanda' OR 'pleito' OR 'juicio' OR 'fraude' OR 'acusado' OR 'delito' OR 'corrupcion' OR 'detenido' OR 'allegado' OR 'cargado' OR 'estafa' OR 'malversacion' OR 'culpable' OR 'carcel' OR 'lavado' OR 'sospecho' OR 'soborno' OR 'desfalco' OR 'desfalcar' OR 'peculado').

2. IWT and Corruption Risks: The Current Picture

This chapter offers an overview of the existing literature on corruption risks and Illegal Wildlife Trade across the countries of focus in this report. This section also showcases the OECD's collection of data on existing corruption incidents reported via the open source data collection exercise.

'There is still a weak treatment in the published evidence of the problems of, and solutions to, wildlife crime from an anti-corruption perspective' (Williams et al., 2016[17]).

Corruption is a major enabling factor in IWT. Yet our knowledge of the precise dimensions and forms this corruption takes is limited. A detailed review of 85 publications reveals that existing published materials on corruption and IWT remain partial and incomplete. The area of study is a recent one: 80% of the reviewed documents were published since 2012. This chapter highlights the knowledge gaps revealed in reviewing the global publicly available literature on IWT and corruption, before zooming in on gaps in the four focus countries. It then considers the gaps revealed from the findings of a mapping exercise of open-source media reporting.

2.1. Taking stock of the evidence

The literature reviewed by the OECD included the output of NGOs, international organisations, academic journals, media outlets and research institutes. The most striking finding was that, of the 85 papers reviewed, only 11 examine the interaction between corruption and IWT specifically. Most others examine IWT more broadly, often focusing on the ways in which poaching and trafficking networks operate, and discussing corruption only tangentially, in that context. A majority of publications make the general observation that IWT and corruption are linked1.

A related finding was that the majority of papers focusing specifically on IWT and corruption approach the issue from an environmental perspective. This echoes the earlier finding by Williams et al. that most research published prior to 2016 examined the nexus through a conservation lens, with anti-corruption specialists having failed to pay the issue comparable attention (Williams et al., 2016[17]). Little has changed in the interim: the existing literature continues to betray limited collaboration between conservation and anti-corruption communities. Testament to this is the considerably smaller number of articles published in governance and criminology journals, relative to conservation-focused outlets – a finding echoing Williams et al.

At the same time, the generally superficial treatment of corruption in the IWT research is revealed by the fact that most papers do not define corruption. Most use corruption as an all-inclusive term, with no attempt to delineate its component parts. Those few that attempt to break it down often use a similar classification to that seen in the broader anti-corruption published material, distinguishing petty from grand corruption (FATF, 2011[20]). A few expand on this to speak of 'political' or 'institutional' corruption in the context of IWT. A limited number seek to draw a conceptual distinction between public and private corruption in the facilitation of IWT (Wyatt and Ngoc Cao, 2015[21]) .

Strikingly, only a small minority of documents reviewed present the results of focused, in-depth research into the dynamics of corruption witnessed or the actors involved (Leader-Williams et al, 2009[22]) (Wyatt and Ngoc Cao, 2015[21]). Although valuable, alone these studies do not paint a comprehensive picture of the nature or extent of corruption enabling IWT across the trade chain. Instead, they provide snapshots of particular dimensions of the nexus, in specific locations, at particular times. As such, in 2016, Williams et al. noted the 'lack [of] a full picture of the types, mechanisms and modalities of corruption in wildlife crime in all locations' (Williams et al., 2016[17]). Little empirical research has been undertaken since into the scale and dynamics of corruption that facilitates IWT.

The little research that does exist is highly focused on particular commodities and locations. In line with the broader literature on IWT, trafficking of ivory and rhino horn from sub-Saharan Africa to East/Southeast Asia dominates in analyses of associated corruption. Very little work exists on corruption linked to trafficking in other forms of wildlife, or to trafficking across other regions, such as Latin America or Europe. In terms of source and transit states, corruption linked to elephant poaching in Tanzania is the most-researched aspect of the relationship. At the other end of the chain, a case study of Vietnam by Wyatt and Ngoc Cao represents the most detailed assessment of the forms corruption takes in consumer markets (Wyatt and Ngoc Cao, 2015[21]). In-depth analyses of the IWT–corruption nexus in consumer markets are largely limited to this study, with little research on China, Hong Kong or other key destination economies.

2.1.1. Tanzania

Of the countries considered in this report, Tanzania has been the subject of greatest (albeit still limited) attention in terms of IWT–corruption linkages. Here, analyses have focused on corruption in the recreational hunting industry (Leader-Williams et al, 2009[22]); corruption-related dismissals from the Ministry of National Resources and Tourism (Vira and Ewign, 2014[23]) and the role of corrupt actors in key trafficking incidents. Alone, these analyses do not provide evidence for greater prevalence of corruption in Tanzania relative to other countries. However, the extent of the poaching and trafficking challenges facing the country is relevant. A 2014 report by the Environmental Investigation Agency (EIA) identified more large ivory flows in Tanzania than any other country (EIA, 2014[24]). Similarly, Vira and Ewing point to the very large amounts of ivory originating from a single source area – the Selous/Niassa ecosystem – noting that these are suggestive of 'a high level of complicity or at the very least inadequate oversight capacity' (Vira and Ewign, 2014[23]) (Sam Wasser et al., 2015[25])[2].

2.1.2. Kenya

Information on IWT–corruption linkages in the other three focus countries is more limited. In Kenya, it has been reported that organised crime has successfully infiltrated national institutions and continues to implicate high-level officials, albeit with few details provided (Vira and Ewign, 2014[23]). Meanwhile, in a 2014 survey of 743 cases of IWT from 2008 to 2013, as many as 70% of case files were reported 'missing' or misplaced by the courts (Kahumbu et al., 2014[26]). Of the cases of the 224 offenders found guilty of wildlife crimes that could be analysed, only 8 (a mere 4%) went to jail. This does not provide definitive evidence of corruption, with little research available to distinguish this from lack of capacity or prioritisation of such cases. Nonetheless, regular reporting of suspensions and arrests of serving officials point to corruption's likely relevance to these figures (Foley, 2014[27]) (Muchangi, 2014[28]). In 2016, a TRAFFIC report on wildlife trafficking in Kenya cited corruption as a significant issue, pointing to the suspension of a magistrate in 2015 over corruption allegations in the course of the prosecution of a major ivory trafficker.

2.1.3. Uganda

Similarly, although Uganda is a transit hub for a range of illegal wildlife products, there are very few substantial examinations of how corruption interacts with IWT. The most detailed is a 2017 study by Cakaj and Lezhnev, which points to a series of alleged instances of corruption linked to trafficking in protected species (Cakaj and Lezhnev, 2017[29]). A study of misconduct among rangers by Moreto et al. also gives useful background knowledge, but does not focus specifically on IWT (Moreto et al., 2015[30]). However, further insight can be gleaned from regular reports by bodies such as the Eco Activists for Governance and Law Enforcement (EAGLE) Network on arrests of officials in connection with IWT. For example, the latter's March 2017 briefing detailed the arrest of 36 wildlife traffickers, including three officials from the army, police and prison authorities (EAGLE Network, 2017[31]). In 2018, a TRAFFIC report spoke of corruption in the court system and at inspection checkpoints, as well as describing the role of exporters as crucial to the corruption process.

2.1.4. Zambia

Little published information is available on corruption as an enabler of IWT in Zambia. Here, available sources are largely limited to infrequent reporting of arrests for trafficking and associated corrupt facilitation. In 2002, for example, EIA pointed to instances of corruption within the then-Zambia Wildlife Authority in South Luangwa National Park (EIA, 2002[32]). In 2010, EIA drew attention to further instances, this time involving arrests of police officers for involvement in ivory and rhino horn trafficking (EIA, 2010[33]).

These sources point mostly to the appearance of specific instances of corruption in each focus country. As such, the existing published material provides merely a selection of snapshots, far from a complete picture of the corruption dynamics at play. Crucial information on the most pressing corruption risks in each case remains absent – as does an analysis of how these dynamics vary by species trafficked, responsible institutions or stage of the supply chain. In seeking to broaden this picture, the OECD analysed the results of open-source media mapping conducted in relation to each focus country.

2.2. Open Source Media Mapping

In an effort to supplement the findings from the literature review, the OECD conducted an open-source mapping exercise of reported cases relating to IWT and corruption. This exercise collated the information currently available from open source reporting on the issues in question. Over 300 reported cases were mapped from 2008-2017, over one third of which were linked to the four focus countries. These break down into 33 cases mapped in relation to Kenya, 27 in relation to Tanzania, 44 in relation to Uganda, and 11 in relation to Zambia. The results were analysed, first, according to the type of wildlife product around which reporting of the offences occurred. Second, they were analysed according to the category of corrupt actor reported to be involved in corruption linked to IWT. Third, the results were broken down according to the status of the offence reported in open-source media.

Figure 2.1 shows the type of wildlife product around which reporting occurred. The findings are striking: 73% of all reported cases of corruption linked to IWT concerned illegal activity around elephant poaching and elephant ivory. A significantly smaller proportion of reported cases were linked to rhino and rhino horn (8%) and pangolin (8%), with 11% of reported cases associated with other wildlife and wildlife products.

Figure 2.1. Species identified in reported corruption cases

Data from open source data collection in the four selected countries in this study

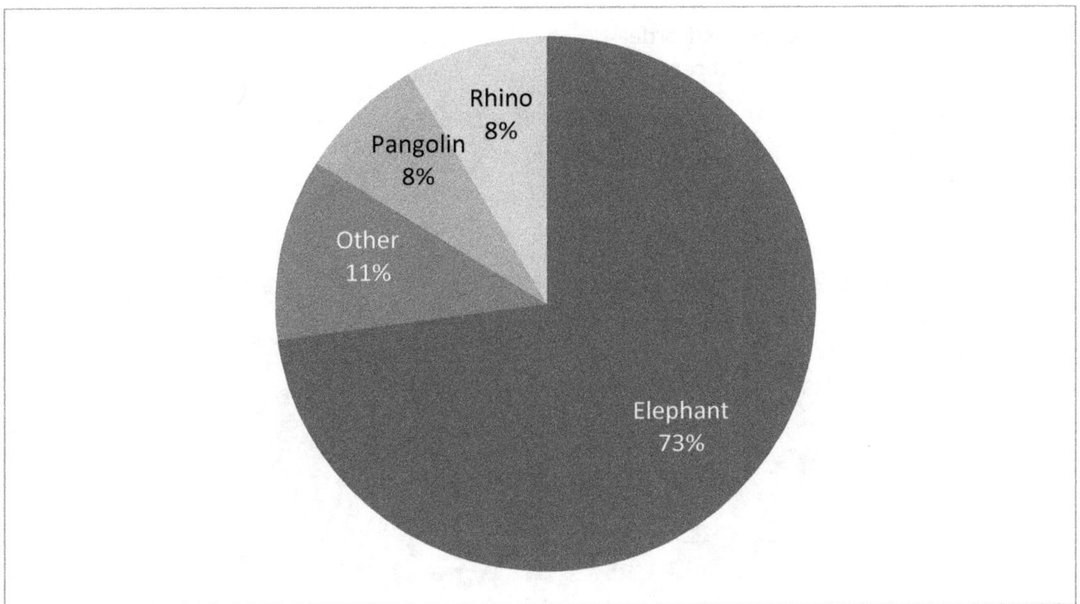

Source: OECD Research

Figure 2.2 shows the category of corrupt actors reportedly involved, broken down by agency or role of the person(s) most often identified in open-source reporting on IWT. In the four focus countries, police officers were reported to be responsible for corruption linked to IWT in the highest number of cases (32%). These were followed by administrative government officials at 19% and, in turn, by military officials – who make up 17% of reported cases. Following this, those persons categorised as forest, game or park rangers were reported to be responsible in only 7% of cases. Elected officials were cited in another 7% of cases, as were foreign officials/diplomats, with customs/border officers cited in a further 6% of cases.

These findings suggest a need to look beyond those perhaps most commonly cited as involved in corruption linked to IWT– namely, mandated wildlife protection officers. However, as noted, these findings are affected by a range of difficulties that limit their reliability. Importantly, given the limited focus on investigating and prosecuting corruption, the majority of corrupt actors likely go unrecorded, and thus unreported in the media. At the same time, it is assumed that reporting of these issues is more extensive in countries with freer civil societies. This factor incorporates a further level of distortion into the results.

Figure 2.2. Agency/Role of Corrupt Actors in Reported Cases

Based on the identifiable agency from open source data collection of the four selected countries in this study

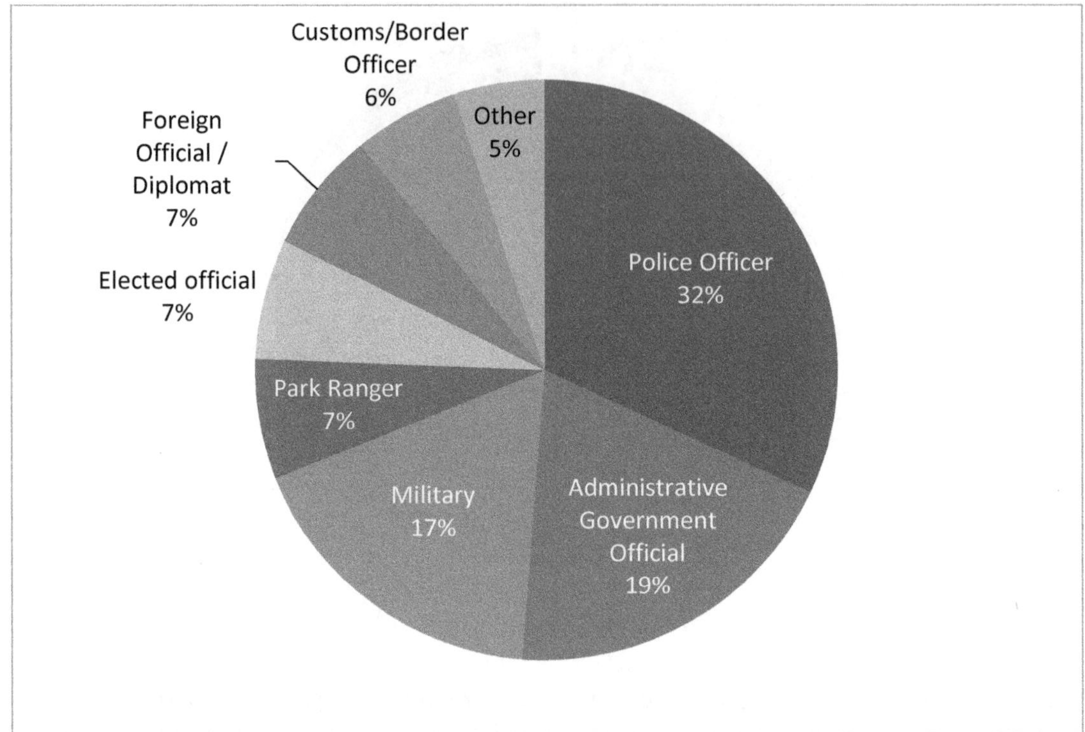

Source: OECD Research.

Such considerations are reinforced when examining the status of the offence reported in open-source media. As shown in Figure 2.3, in as many as 59% of articles, reporting was based on arrests or charges for corruption linked to IWT. Here, there is an inevitable bias towards coverage of minor offences that are more easily uncovered and charged by law enforcement. Typically, these include illegal possession of wildlife products by ground-level officers. In this context, large numbers of higher level offences are likely to go unreported.

Meanwhile, the findings in relation to events after arrest suggest that follow up reporting rarely occurs. Additional analysis conducted of the arrest or charge revealed that the majority of reports in the media did not follow-up on the subsequent stages of prosecution or sentencing after the report of the arrest. Strikingly, as figure 2.3. indicates, only 3% of media reports cover convictions for corruption-related offences. This echoes the findings of court monitoring conducted in Kenya, in which the cases of only 4% of wildlife crime offenders analysed from 2008-13 saw the accused imprisoned.

Figure 2.3. Status of Case at Time of Report

Data collection from the four selected countries in this study

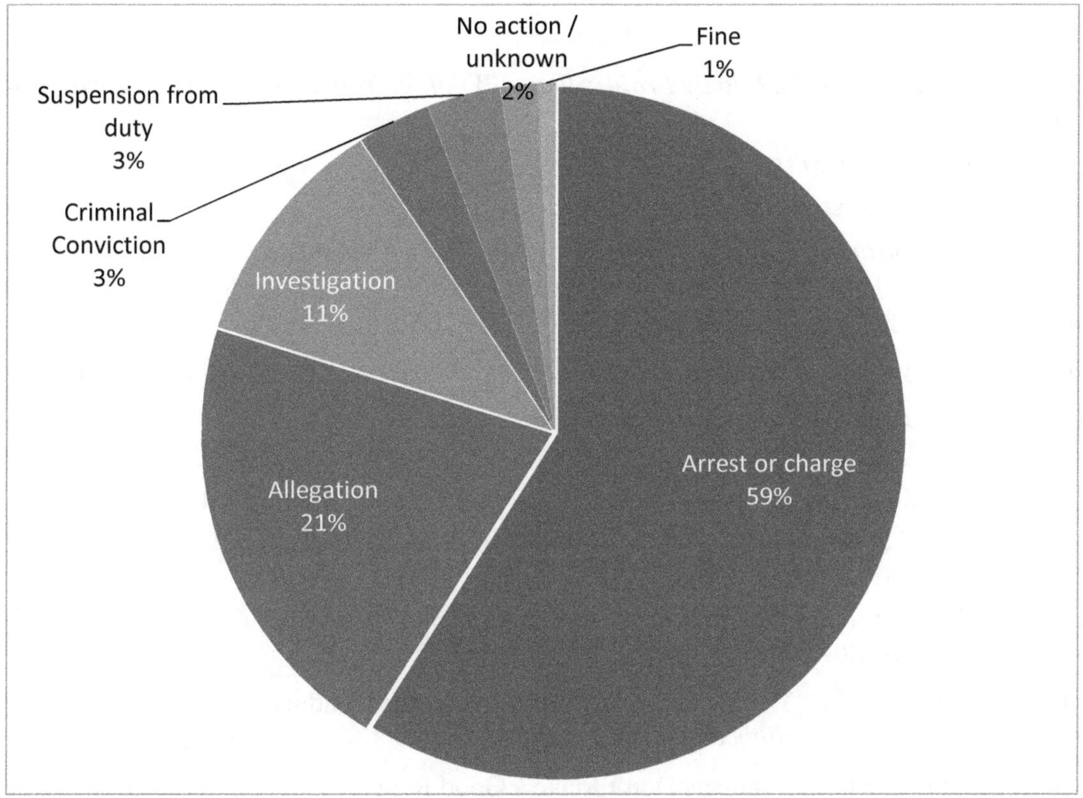

Source: OECD research.

The data reported in the figures above is useful to indicate the breakdown of publicly reported corruption incidents. The limited scope of the information is clear, however, with results limited to those cases on which journalists have felt able to report. At the same time, the bias of this data is evident, particularly insofar as it favours reporting of low-level forms of corruption.

In an attempt to widen the available information beyond what is visible from existing publicly available evidence and open-source media mapping, the rest of this paper presents the findings from 90 semi-structured interviews in the focus countries. These were designed to collect as-yet largely undocumented practitioner and other expert knowledge on the most prevalent corruption risks seen in each case. Risks are organised according to two overarching sets of influencing variables. These include institutional factors, which are examined in Chapter 3, and supply-chain factors, examined in Chapter 4. Institutional factors are presented first, in an effort to set the scene for the specific supply-chain factors examined subsequently. Following this, Chapter 5 presents findings in relation to the most effective proposed responses.

References

Cakaj, L. and S. Lezhnev (2017), *Deadly Profits: Illegal Wildlife Trafficking through Uganda and South Sudan*.

EAGLE Network (2017), *Wildlife Law Enforcement Briefing*, http://www.eagle-enforcement.org/data/files/eagle-briefing-march-03-2017-public.pdf.

EIA (2002), *Back in Business: Elephant Poaching and the Ivory Black Markets of Asia.*, http://dx.doi.org/Back in Business: Elephant Poaching and the Ivory Black Markets of Asia', 2002, p. 4 https://eia-international.org/wp-content/uploads/Back-in-Business-2002.pdf.

EIA (2014), *Vanishing Point: Criminality, Corruption and the Devastation of Tanzania's Elephants*.

FATF (2011), *Laundering the Proceeds of Corruption*, http://www.fatf-gafi.org/media/fatf/documents/reports/Laundering%20the%20Proceeds%20of%20Corruption.pdf.

Foley, J. (2014), "Kenyan Gov. to Oversee Wildlife Service Amid Corruption Allegations", http://www.natureworldnews.com/articles/6593/20140411/kenyan-gov-to-oversee-wildlife-service-amid-corruption-allegations.htm, accessed 13 February 2018.

Kahumbu et al. (2014), *Scoping Study on the Prosecution of Wildlife Related Crimes in Kenyan Courts: January 2008 to June 2013*, http://www.thedswt.org.uk/wildlifecrimekenya.pdf.

Leader-Williams et al (2009), "The Influence of Corruption on the Conduct of Recreational Hunting", *Conservation and Rural Livelihoods: Science and Practice*.

Moreto et al. (2015), "Such Misconducts Don't Make a Good Ranger: Examining Law Enforcement Ranger Wrongdoing in Uganda", *British Journal of Criminology*, Vol. 55/2, pp. William D Moreto et al., 'Such Misconducts Don't Make a Good Ranger: Examining Law Enforcement Ranger Wrongdoing in Uganda', British Journal of Criminology, https://academic.oup.com/bjc/article/55/2/359/596454.

Muchangi, J. (2014), *Kenya: KWS Suspends Six Top Officers Over Poaching*, http://allafrica.com/stories/201404110399.html?aa_source=slideout.

Sam Wasser et al. (2015), *Genetic Assignment of Large Seizures of Elephant Ivory Reveals Africa's Major Poaching Hotspots*, Science.

TRAFFIC (2016), *Strengthening the arm of the law through judicial training*, http://www.traffic.org/home/2016/5/25/strengthening-the-arm-of-the-law-through-judicial-training.htm

TRAFFIC (2007), *Forestry, governance and national development: Lessons learned from a logging boom in southern Tanzania*, TRAFFIC East/Southern Africa.

USAID (2015), *Wildlife Crime in Indonesia: A Rapid Assessment of the Current Knowledge, Trends and Priority Actions', Changes for Justice Project*, http://pdf.usaid.gov/pdf_docs/PA00KH52.pdf.

US FWS (2018), *U.S. Fish & Wildlife Service: The illegal wildlife trade*, https://www.fws.gov/international/travel-and-trade/illegal-wildlife-trade.html.

Vira, V. and T. Ewign (2014), *Ivory's Curse: The Militarization & Professionalization of Poaching in Africa*, https://www.all-creatures.org/articles/ar-Ivorys-Curse-2014.pdf.

Wyatt, T. and A. Ngoc Cao (2015), "Corruption and Wildlife Trafficking", *U4 Issue*, Vol. No 11, http://www.u4.no/publications/corruption-and-wildlife-trafficking/.

Notes

[1] An illustrative example where corruption is referred to as a 'key barrier' to combating IWT in Indonesia, but the issue is not addressed in any further detail (USAID, 2015[162]).

[2] Researchers Wasser et al. at Washington State University have identified southeast Tanzania and northern Mozambique, specifically the Selous/Niassa ecosystem, as the source of 86–93% of savannah elephant ivory found in large seizures made between 2006 and 2014.

3. IWT and Corruption Risks: Institutional Factors

This chapter conducts an analysis of the wildlife management and conservation authorities' structures, and the enforcement and corruption gaps across the focus countries. This section also highlights the risks and vulnerabilities in the criminal justice system and the gaps in public accountability that may lead to heightened risks from corruption.

Corruption risks play a major role in structuring wildlife conservation policies and management systems in many African countries. It is a natural resource, similar to timber precious stones and minerals or oil, that can attract illegal activity or corrupt governing practices (Nelson, 2009[34]). When considering corruption linked to IWT in the focus countries, it is crucial to assess how the nature of existing institutional frameworks affects – and is affected by – corruption risks. By breaking down these institutional factors, we can then parcel out the findings and recommendations offered to actors engaged in institutional reform, or in other structural interventions in the focus countries' wildlife sectors.

For this section, the OECD research team interviewed 90 respondents to elicit knowledge and perspectives on key institutional factors, with vulnerabilities to corruption drawn out in specific cases. Respondents cited three broad sets of vulnerabilities most frequently:

- Gaps in core public integrity institutions' frameworks
- Corruption risks facing wildlife management authorities
- Institutional vulnerabilities in the criminal justice system

From these three angles, we can consider a more structured approach to the study of corruption risks that institutions face, and subsequently, the formulation of recommendations on how to address each one.

3.1. Gaps in Core Public Integrity Frameworks

Anti-corruption agencies are responsible for overseeing public sector activities that range from core public service delivery to procurement using a range of targeted mechanisms, such as developing high standards for public officials, ensuring that the appropriate legislative provisions are in place, and most importantly, implementing, monitoring and enforcing the anti-corruption architecture across all government administrations.

The UN Convention against Corruption (UNCAC) is the general framework for fighting corruption. In line with the Convention, each country maintains specific legislation criminalising a range of corruption offences. Kenya, Tanzania, Uganda and Zambia have all signed and ratified the UNCAC.

This legislation is embodied principally in the Anti-Corruption and Economic Crimes Act, 2003 in Kenya; the Prevention and Combating of Corruption Act, 2007 in Tanzania; the Anti-Corruption Act, 2009 in Uganda; and the Anti-Corruption Act, 2012 in Zambia. Each country periodically submits to the mechanism for the Review of Implementation of UNCAC. In line with this, the UNCAC mandates country visits and the issuance of specific recommendations for strengthening criminalisation and law enforcement, international cooperation and other key components of UNCAC.

All four countries have dedicated anti-corruption authorities whose institutional responsibilities are to strengthen the effectiveness of the public sector by mitigating corruption risks and enforcing infractions. The mandated authorities are:

- The Ethics and Anti-Corruption Commission (EACC) in Kenya;
- The Prevention and Combating of Corruption Bureau (PCCB) in Tanzania;
- The Inspectorate of Government (IG) in Uganda; and
- The Anti-Corruption Commission (ACC) in Zambia.

Anti-corruption authorities should be responsible for developing a coherent and comprehensive integrity system that is inclusive of all relevant agencies, promotes a culture of public integrity among the public sector, and importantly, assures accountability for the public sector (OECD, 2017[35]).[1]

The below section identifies several gaps with the role of core integrity agencies and the transmission of anti-corruption frameworks to achieve a whole of government approach that reaches wildlife authorities. Principally, evidence suggests a generally weak institutional collaboration between anti-corruption and wildlife management authorities and a weak application of core public sector anti-corruption principles (OECD, 2017[35]). As a result, wildlife management authorities in the countries surveyed have not developed effective systems to prevent and detect corruption in remote areas where anti-corruption agencies are not present. Within society, there are issues with the cultural acceptability of corruption relative to the wildlife sector as well due to perceptions of low social and economic costs of IWT. Finally, accountability and enforcement remains low due to infrequent investigations of public officials and inconsistent or light sanctions. However, encouragingly, there have been recent shifts in the approaches to corruption in the countries studied. High-level enforcement cases have recently taken place in some countries, and there are encouraging signs that civil society and other watchdogs are participating more actively to assure accountability that is more thorough. Nonetheless, numerous gaps remain that need to be addressed.

3.1.1. Anti-corruption and the Wildlife Management Authorities

In considering structural determiners of corruption risk, numerous respondents cited the limited penetration of the public sector integrity mechanisms into the wildlife and conservation sector. Across all focus countries, respondents noted a broad lack of focus on anti-corruption from within the wildlife management authorities, and conversely, a broad lack of focus on IWT by relevant anti-corruption authorities. As noted by one respondent, 'dealing with poachers is not a core priority for the anti-corruption agency' (GA-08, 2017[36]). In at least one focus country, respondents from the anti-corruption authority also noted that 'no cases of corruption linked to IWT had ever been brought, with none pending' (GA-04, 2017[37]).

In one country, anti-corruption authorities had received numerous indications that direct communication between officials and poachers are taking place (GA-04, 2017[37]). However, the respondent in question noted that these had not been acted on, as other issues relating to public integrity are given greater priority. In addition, few anti-corruption offices have specific expertise in environmental matters (NG-18, 2017[38]) (NG-20, 2017[39]). In many cases, for action to be taken or prioritisation systems changed, anti-corruption authorities observed the need for higher-level prioritisation. This brings the issue back to political will, and the perceived harm – including to citizens themselves – caused by IWT.

Indeed, scarce resources are often cited as an issue from the anti-corruption authorities. Certainly, corruption is prevalent across multiple sectors, as indicated by the four countries' scores on Transparency International's Corruption Perceptions Index (Transparency International, 2017[40]). In this context, the question of prioritisation arises. Decisions must be made around where to focus limited resources, with anti-corruption authorities unable to address corruption in all areas of the public sector where it may occur (GA-04, 2017[37]) (GA-10, 2017[41]) (NG-20, 2017[39]) (IO-02, 2017[42]).

In some cases, political will has been forthcoming. In Tanzania, the PCCB has not traditionally focused on IWT, prioritising instead corruption in other sectors. However, a dedicated branch has now begun to examine corruption exclusively within the environmental sector. This policy shift has been conducted thanks to greater awareness and recognition of the high economic and social cost of IWT (GA-05, 2017[43]) (GA-07, 2017[44]) (GA-08, 2017[36]) (IO-02, 2017[42]).

In Uganda, meanwhile, respondents noted that the IG had investigated the wildlife management authority more often than other government agencies (GA-13, 2017[45]). They did so pointing to an ongoing, high-level investigation into the wildlife management authority. Specifically, in May 2017, the Ugandan President requested the IG to investigate eight specific areas of suspected corruption and mismanagement within the authority (Box 3.1). However, a number of respondents cast doubt on the potential outcome of the UWA investigation. They did so pointing to a previous suspension of the then-executive director over the 2014 discovery of a large ivory stockpile theft (NG-18, 2017[38]) (NG-20, 2017[39]) (Mafabi, 2017[46]). This ultimately led only to his reinstatement; meanwhile, to date, no one has been held accountable for the ivory theft. At the same time, as noted by Cakaj and Lezhnev, there have been 'other cases of officers that were not prosecuted, other cases stalled in the court system, and [of] judges … reportedly harassed over wildlife cases' (Cakaj and Lezhnev, 2017[29]).

Respondents also questioned whether the IG had been adequately resourced to conduct such a high-level, wide-reaching corruption investigation (NG-18, 2017[38]) (NG-20, 2017[39]). In addition, they questioned the extent to which specific findings or recommendations would be acted on in concrete terms (NG-18, 2017[38]) (NG-20, 2017[39]). However, Cakaj and Lezhnev observe that 'an investigation ordered by the president himself, combined with the new wildlife court, may mark a policy shift. It will be important to watch what happens with these investigations and if indeed prosecutions and convictions result from them' (Cakaj and Lezhnev, 2017[29]).

Box 3.1. President Orders Investigation into UWA in Uganda

In May 2017, the Ugandan President wrote to the Inspector General of Government ordering a high-level investigation into the activities of the then-executive director of UWA (Mafabi, 2017[47]). In his letter, the President ordered the IG to investigate UWA for eight possible crimes or counts of mismanagement. These included, notably, the reported loss of wildlife trophies from its storeroom; reported complicity with Chinese diplomats in ivory trafficking from DRC, CAR and South Sudan; and the reported issuance of licences to sell pangolin scales in contravention of international conventions.

The letter also referenced alleged attempted bribery of banks. According to the letter, the then-executive director 'also tried to get bribes from Centenary Bank, DFCU and Crane Bank so as to maintain the shs28 billion deposits in those banks (Namugerwa, 2017[48]).' 'When the banks refused to bribe him', the letter continues, 'he withdrew the money from the banks and caused a loss of shs 1.5 billion'. The then-executive director is alleged to have denied these allegations, noting that the funds derived from the sale of gorilla permits, and that decisions around them were vested in the board of trustees, rather than the executive director (Namugerwa, 2017[48]) .

At time of writing, the outcome of the investigation was not known. However, the accusations around collusion with Chinese diplomats had sparked diplomatic tension. This saw the Chinese Ambassador to Uganda protest the contents of the letter and a spokesperson for the Chinese Foreign Affairs Ministry dismiss the allegations as 'totally unfounded' (Kaaya, 2017[49]). The accusation was later publicly retracted by the Ugandan government (Bwire, 2017[50]).

It must be noted that this investigation largely concerns alleged corruption at the strategic and institutional levels. When it comes to investigating corruption at the lower, operational levels, the anti-corruption authority – in Uganda and other focus countries – has typically been less involved (GA-13, 2017[45]) (NG-18, 2017[38]) (NG-20, 2017[39]) (IE-04, 2017[51]). In several countries, this is attributed to an often-reactive stance on the part of the anti-corruption authority. Here, the picture painted was one of overstretched anti-corruption authorities acting largely on public referrals in relation to perceived lower-level instances – rather than regularly undertaking proactive investigations from early detection systems or risk-assessments (GA-18, 2017[52]) (NG-20, 2017[39]).

Accountability of officials engaged in the wildlife sector is also more difficult to assure, as the public service deliveries linked to IWT often take place in remote, rural areas, away from population centres. In this respect, public accountability and transparency are more difficult to assure through open government methods and practises. The risks from un-reported corruption is therefore more pronounced in rurally based wildlife sectors than in other public-facing sectors (such as health, education and politics) (NG-23, 2017[53]) (NG-20, 2017[39]). At the same time, society's public awareness of the true harms and cost of IWT are generally not well recognized, and this may further discourage public reporting.

For example, Zambia's Anti-Corruption Commission reports low levels of engagement from whistle-blowers or community referrals for IWT (GA-18, 2017[52]) (NG-22,

2017[54]) (IE-05, 2017[55]). In the case where public reports are made, these typically involve hunting concessions or licensing of parks and reserves. Little information is said to be regularly received in relation to wildlife trafficking itself, and the Commission is said to do limited proactive investigation of IWT-linked cases (GA-18, 2017[52]) (NG-22, 2017[54]) (IE-05, 2017[55]).

Box 3.2. Zambia's Former Anti-Corruption Commission Species Protection Unit

Until it was recently dissolved, a dedicated Species Protection Unit existed within the Commission since 1980. The unit adopted a proactive approach to preventing and investigating corruption specifically within the wildlife sector (GA-18, 2017[60]) (IE-05, 2017[95]).

Among other actions, the unit launched public awareness campaigns via radio and other means, warning of the harms of IWT and encouraging reporting. The unit also provided training to wildlife management authority staff and maintained staff at Lusaka's international airport. The initiative is reported to have led to significant volumes of reporting on IWT-related corruption, before the unit was disbanded and reporting again fell (GA-18, 2017[60]) (IE-05, 2017[95]).

Wildlife authorities reported that if discovered through internal processes, corruption cases are nearly always be treated as a disciplinary issue, rather than one following procedures that may involve anti-corruption authorities (GA-04, 2017[37]) (GA-19, 2017[56]). As observed in one focus country, 'the wildlife protection authorities largely seek to deal with corruption internally and does not invite the anti-corruption authority to assist' (GA-12, 2017[57]). Other respondents echoed these findings, citing the lack of incentives for wildlife management authorities to deal with corruption through external mechanisms. In such a scenario, concerns around the risks to an agency – or particular unit's – external reputation are often an important part of the consideration. Instead, standard responses may include internal transfer to different or less desirable posts or, in some cases, dismissal (GA-19, 2017[56]) (NG-06, 2017[58]) (NG-21, 2017[59]).

3.1.2. Internal Integrity Mechanisms

According to the OECD's Directorate for Public Governance, codes of conduct for the public sector are used to ensure that civil servants and public officials "serve public interests with impartiality, legality, integrity and transparency on a daily basis". Countries may implement supplementary codes for specific areas that are known to be exposed to heightened integrity risks. The OECD notes, "Ideally, codes combine aspirational values and more detailed standards on how to put them into practice" (OECD, 2018[60]).

In discussions across focus countries, it was noted that most standards and ethics codes are not focused on corrupt activities related to the sale of illegal wildlife products or facilitation of IWT. Instead, codes of ethics refer to general risks, such as employment and benefits fraud or procurement fraud (IO-01, 2017[61]) (IO-02, 2017[42]) (NG-03, 2017[62]).

Implementing codes of conduct and monitoring compliance infractions are also reported to be hindered by a lack of general dedicated resources, and due to the decentralized posting of wildlife officials. In Zambia, for example, a code of conduct exists within the DNPW conservation authority. However, accountability is limited, as no internal body is charged with monitoring and promoting this code (GA-17-2017, 2017[63]) (GA-19, 2017[56]). While respondents noted that an Integrity Committee exists at the Zambian Ministry level, no equivalent is yet present within the department itself (GA-17-2017, 2017[63]) (GA-19, 2017[56]).

Upon consideration of the above-noted integrity gaps among wildlife and conservation authorities, the risk of detection for corrupt actors is low and the likelihood of impunity for misconduct is high. In this context, potentially corrupt actors (particularly in the field) do not face significant risks from internal integrity mechanisms or external investigations from national anti-corruption administrations. Instead, when public officials are caught, they are tried as any member of the public, rather than as a public official entrusted with maintaining public trust. This gap analysis points to serious shortfalls in the assurance of public sector integrity among wildlife Management authorities. As evidence of the gaps in prevention and enforcement, across the focus countries, reports of violations and involvement of officers in IWT cases are common, meanwhile convictions for crimes related corruption for IWT remain in the single digits – in some, not one could be cited.

Box 3.3. Convictions of Conservation Officials related to IWT

Below are several cases in which serving officers have been convicted for crimes linked to the sale or facilitation of IWT, but have not been found guilty of violations for breach of public trust, bribery, or other related corruption offences:

UPDF Officers Convicted in Uganda

On 24 March 2016, police arrested two Uganda People's Defence Force (UPDF) officers in possession of 12 pieces of ivory worth Shs 129 million. A Corporal of the Special Forces Command and a Major attached to the Chieftaincy of Military Intelligence, Mbuya Army Headquarters, were intercepted by police posing as buyers at the Hotel Africana in Kampala.

In February 2017, the pair were found guilty of unlawful possession of protected species, accepting the transfer of protected species, and conspiracy to commit an offence of illegal possession of protected species. They were sentenced, by a wildlife court established in Uganda in October 2016, to a fine of 4 million Ugandan shillings (approximately $1,100).

Police Officers Convicted in Tanzania

In September 2017, eight individuals – including two police officers – were convicted by Tanzania's High Court for illegal possession of 70 ivory tusks. The tusks were estimated to be worth over 850 million Tanzanian shillings (approximately $370,000).

All of the accused were found guilty of possession of government trophies contrary to Section 86 of the Wildlife Conservation Act, 2009. On this count, they were sentenced to 20 years and ordered to pay a fine if 8.5 billion Tanzanian shillings.

In addition, the police officers were found guilty on a second count under Section 57 and 60 of the Economic and Organised Crime Control Act, 2009. For intentionally promoting and furthering the objectives of a criminal organisation by acquiring and possessing 70 elephant tusks, they were sentenced to a further 15 years (although this sentence will run concurrently with the first). The Senior Magistrate responsible for the case noted that five witnesses and a range of exhibits brought before the Kibaha Resident Magistrate's Court – from the ivory itself to the Kauzeni Check Point register and identity cards – provided abundant evidence of the two officers' involvement. In addition, the court ordered the confiscation of the vehicles used to transport the ivory.

Zambian Defence Force Officer Convicted in Malawi

On 2 September 2016, a Zambian Defence Force captain was arrested, along with two others, in the Malawian border town of Mchinji. They were charged with dealing in government trophies and illegal possession of three elephant tusks as well as lion and leopard skins believed to have been sourced in Zambia's South Luangwa National Park.

On 30 September 2016, the Lilongwe Magistrate Court found all three guilty of illegal possession, sentencing them to 40 months in jail, with no option of a fine given. The case was praised by conservationists in Malawi as the first concluded case under a newly funded public-private litigation project for serious cases of wildlife crime.

Sources: (Cakaj and Lezhnev, 2017[29]) (Ndagire, 2017[64]) (Daily News Tanzania, 2017[65]) (Jamiyeto, 2016[66]) (Lilongwe Wildlife Trust, 2016[67])

In the few cases in which officials have been convicted (see Box 3.4) prosecutors pursue charges for illegal possession or sale – as they would be for any normal poacher or trafficker. An exception to this is the case of two police officers in Tanzania convicted under both the Wildlife Conservation Act and the Economic and Organised Crime Control Act (Box 3.5). In general, limited focus is placed on 'tracing back' the chain of corruption that led to a seizure, or pursuing a broader criminal charge. Across the focus countries, no case could be cited of indirect facilitation or of public officers who were tried under anti-corruption law.

3.1.3. The Role of Civil Society and the Media

The OECD's 2017 Recommendation on public integrity notes the value of ensuring a whole of society culture on public integrity. The recommendations also encourage a society that includes "watchdog organisations, citizens groups, labour unions and independent media to encourage transparency and engage a wider range of stakeholders in the delivery of public services" (OECD, 2017[35]). Respondents in all countries echoed this perspective, noting the potential value of society's engagement in countering corruption and the role that civil society can play in bridging the structural gaps that feature above. Indeed, public awareness and knowledge of the plight and cost of IWT can foster constructive engagement from civil society. There are however a number of factors that can affect public opinion or cultural norms. For example, cultural habits and the capture of the public discussion from certain actors seeking to co-opt public opinion, and a general lack of awareness of the cost of IWT among society can limit the impact of civil society's engagement.

Poaching can be a domestic source of luxury products for consumption in local markets – thus limiting public opposition. In countries such as Zambia, bush meat consumption derived from poaching is widely held to be a luxury that can denote status. Bush meat continues to be widely consumed – including at high-level functions, and gatherings such as weddings and celebrations among the growing urban middle class (GA-19, 2017[56]) (FD-05, 2017[68]) (NG-21, 2017[59]).

High-level disinterest in IWT can also undermine momentum within civil society. In Zambia, in October 2011, six hundred prisoners, many of whom had been serving time for IWT related offences, were reportedly pardoned and released on the grounds that such crimes did not pose a significant public risk (Lusaka Times, 2011[69]). As noted by one author, the pardon sends 'an unmistakeable message' to any Zambians thinking of hunting an impala for the pot that the consequences will be limited (Allison, 2011[70]). In such cases, there is limited "blow back" from media or the general public, as the perceived cost of IWT are not well known, and the economic harms (through for example, losses in tourism revenue) are poorly communicated to the public.

Respondents across the focus countries noted the critical role of independent media interest in reducing corruption risks. Respondents indicated that media coverage of IWT prosecutions, for example, serves two purposes. First, it can make it clear that wildlife-related law can be effectively enforced, thus raising the deterrent facing traffickers and corrupt facilitators. Secondly, it can increase transparency and accountability where actors across the criminal justice system attempt to quietly bury cases – by holding those responsible accountable. Exemplifying this latter approach, several NGOs use an 'eyes in the courtroom' approach in an effort to shine a public spotlight on dubious decisions during trials (GA-09, 2017[71]) (GA-12, 2017[57]) (NG-01, 2017[72]) (NG-13, 2017[73]) (NG-21, 2017[59]) (GA-21, 2017[74]).

In Uganda, Tanzania and, most notably, Kenya, civil society have been more active in their engagement. In Kenya, the media spotlight on the trial of a high-level wildlife trafficker was closely followed by the public and NGOs. NGOs provided a constant watching brief at the trial – part of a broader programme of courtroom monitoring to engage public opinion and hold the prosecution and courts to account. In the case in question, the high-level trafficker was sentenced to 20 years in jail, but recently was released due to inconsistencies in the prosecution's case (Kahumbu, 2016[75]). While the initial conviction demonstrates that effective public pressure can help to mitigate corruption during the trial, the recent quashing of the conviction due to gaps in the prosecution illustrates that eyes in the courtroom are only one pillar in the broader architecture of public integrity. Institutional vulnerabilities such as those recently seen in this case are discussed in the criminal justice system are discussed section 3.3 below.

The situation in countries like Uganda and Tanzania reveals the impact of increasing public consciousness around IWT-linked corruption. In Tanzania, substantial media coverage has surrounded the ongoing case of a Chinese wildlife trafficker, arrested in October 2015. As noted by one respondent, increased media interest in corruption and IWT is linked to 'growing recognition of the threat to wildlife as an economic sector, and as the country's main source of foreign exchange' (RI-01, 2017[76]). This rise of public consciousness is thought to have been triggered by public concern around the dramatic elephant losses witnessed since the mid-2000s, and effective reporting of these losses to the public. In Uganda, meanwhile, a spate of media stories was published around the 2014 theft of 1.35 tons of ivory from UWA stockpile rooms.

However, many respondents also noted that the media is itself not impervious to corruption, or being co-opted. In some cases, respondents noted, 'the media has been corrupted to report the other side of a story playing out in court' (GA-09, 2017[71]). In doing so, 'the aim is to evoke public sympathy with the accused, thus diminishing public pressure to convict'. Concerns of this nature were raised in all focus countries, with this corruption risk extending beyond the wildlife domain.

In sum, whether in the courts or wildlife management authorities of the country in question, respondents highlighted opportunities for corruption across nearly all institutions involved in preventing, investigating or prosecuting IWT. The corruption risks facing each become most concerning when accountability and transparency are reduced. This may occur as a function of any of – or a combination of – the prevailing structural conditions discussed in this section. In engaging with institutions across the chain, these risks should be considered carefully by all those looking to promote organizational or structural reform. Such efforts can be complemented by effective engagement with civil society, as part of broader efforts to raise awareness of the economic, social and environmental harms of corruption and IWT.

3.2. Corruption Risks Facing Wildlife Management Authorities

The respondents interviewed identified a number of corruption risks affecting wildlife management authorities, often relating to their position within each country's broader institutional architecture. These vulnerabilities vary depending on the particular role – and the unique structural features – of each wildlife management authority. To assess these, a clear understanding of the focus countries' approaches to wildlife governance is required. Across all four countries, arrangements differ in terms of the degree of decentralisation of wildlife governance structures, including those to manage wildlife use rights, among others. Each structure offers strengths and weaknesses when it comes to particular corruption risks.

All four countries studied have national wildlife management authorities mandated to conserve and manage wildlife. In Kenya, the relevant institution is the Kenya Wildlife Service (KWS), a parastatal body with responsibility for managing 8% of the country's land – comprising 23 National Parks, 28 National Reserves, four National Sanctuaries, as well as Marine National Parks and Reserves (KWS, 2018[77])[2]. In Uganda, responsibility for wildlife protection sits with the Uganda Wildlife Authority (UWA), a semi-autonomous agency managing 10 national parks, 12 wildlife reserves and 14 wildlife sanctuaries, under the Ministry of Wildlife, Tourism and Antiquities (UWA,(n.d.)[78]). In Zambia, the relevant body is the Department of National Parks and Wildlife (DNPW), a government agency under the Ministry of Tourism charged with managing 20 National Parks and 35 Game Management Areas.

In Tanzania, a larger number of agencies bear wildlife management responsibilities. The Tanzania National Parks Authority (TANAPA) runs the country's 16 national parks, while the Ngorongoro Conservation Area Authority (NCAA) forms the management body for the Ngorongoro Conservation Area. Historically, the Wildlife Division was responsible for wildlife beyond the authority of TANAPA and NCAA, covering 28 Game Reserves and 38 Game Controlled Areas. However, in May 2014, the government established the Tanzania Wildlife Management Authority (TAWA) to 'take over the wildlife management functions … currently performed by the Wildlife Division' (URT, 2017[79]). The Wildlife Division is now described as leading on strategic sectoral coordination (GA-07, 2017[44]). At the same time, the National Taskforce Anti-Poaching (NTAP) comprises a multi-agency unit charged with intelligence-led law enforcement and prosecution of IWT.

In all four focus countries, wildlife management authorities are responsible for upholding national legislation on wildlife conservation and wildlife trade. The Wildlife Conservation and Management Act of 2013 embodies this legislation in Kenya; the 2009 Wildlife Conservation Act, and 2002 National Parks Act in Tanzania; the 1996 Wildlife Act in Uganda; and the 2015 Wildlife Act in Zambia. These acts vary in the extent to which they fully satisfy the requirements for implementation of CITES. As a result, in some countries, legislative amendment processes are underway. In Uganda, for example, a strengthened Uganda Wildlife Bill 2017 is under review in an effort address legislative loopholes (EIA, 2016[80]).

Table 3.1. Relevant Conservation Authorities in Focus Countries

	Kenya	Tanzania	Uganda	Zambia
Relevant Conservation Authority(s)	Kenya Wildlife Service (KWS)	Tanzania National Parks Authority (TANAPA) Ngoro Ngoro Conservation Area (NCAA) Tanzania Wildlife Management Authority (TAWA)	Uganda Wildlife Authority (UWA)	Department of National Parks and Wildlife (DNPW),
Management Responsibilities	23 National Parks, 28 National Reserves, 4 National Sanctuaries,	16 national parks (TANAPA) 1 national Park (NCAA) covering 28 Game Reserves and 38 Game Controlled Areas (TAWA)	10 national parks, 12 wildlife reserves and 14 wildlife sanctuaries	20 National Parks and 35 Game Management Areas
% of total landmass under responsibility as protected areas	8%	28%	13%	31%
Relevant legislation	Wildlife Conservation and Management Act of 2013	the 2009 Wildlife Conservation Act, 2002 National Parks Act in Tanzania	the 1996 Wildlife Act Uganda Wildlife Bill 2017 (pending)	2015 Wildlife Act in Zambia
Organisational Structure	Parastatal (State) corporation	Parastatal, under Ministry of Wildlife, Tourism and Antiquities	Parastatal, under Ministry of Natural Resources and Tourism (MNRT)	Parastatal under the Ministry of Tourism, Environment and Natural Resources
Primary responsibility for preventing and disrupting poaching incidents (Y/N)	Yes	Yes	Yes	Yes
Direct contribution of Tourism and Travel as a % of GDP (Price, 2017[81])	3.71%	4.65%	1.85%	6.5% (est.)
Top 3 most visited parks (Price, 2017[81])	Lake Nakuru Tsavo (East) Amboseli	Serengeti Lake Manyara Tarangire	Murchison Falls Queen Elizabeth Lake Mburo	South Luangwa Mosi-oa-Tunya Klower Zambezi
Combined estimated annual number of visitors in top 3 parks (Price, 2017[81])	78,000 (2015)	162,000 (2015)	690,000 (2012)	350,000 (2015)

In enforcing this legislation across the focus countries, national wildlife management structures bear a number of distinct organisational commonalities. When discussing structural vulnerabilities to corruption in all focus countries, many interviewees pointed to the significant vertical reach of wildlife management authorities relative to other government agencies. This owes to the front-line, ground-level responsibility they hold for wildlife protection and combating IWT. In each country, wildlife management authorities hold primary responsibility for preventing and disrupting poaching incidents across vast protected and other source areas. To meet this responsibility, wildlife management authorities deploy significant numbers of field-level law enforcement officers across often-remote, wildlife-rich areas.

The HQ-to-field extension creates a string of vulnerabilities with respect to corruption. The reach of wildlife management agencies' remits across remote, rural locations puts often-vast distances between superiors in capital-based headquarters and front-line officers in far-flung reserves. As remarked by Moreto et al. (referring to the case of Uganda), a crucial structural enabler of corruption lies in the 'considerable amount of discretion' enjoyed by rangers, who 'operate outside the direct gaze of their supervisors' (Moreto et al., 2015[30]). Respondents noted that the often significant distance between field officers and management creates a unique structural vulnerability to corruption.

3.2.1. Rotation of Officers

Human resource (HR) management in a fair, open and transparent system of hiring and managing officials is an essential pillar in countering corruption risks. A system that mitigates abuses of position and sets clear rules and administrative procedures is essential in high-risk areas such as in wildlife management authorities (OECD, 2017[35]). For example, rotation policies are used to move field officers between locations. In all countries visited, wildlife management authorities are also expected to rotate field and HQ-based staff on a regular basis. Respondents in all four countries noted that these rotational structures are crucial to reducing the corruption risks that arise particularly where field officers form bonds over time with local communities.

However, a number of respondents pointed to discrepancies in the rigour with which such policies are enforced. A number of interviewees pointed to numerous requests granted to individual rangers and wardens to remain longer than standard rotation policies allow in preferred locations (GA-01, 2017[82]). According to interviews with sources familiar with these policies, criminal networks are able to exploit this flexibility in enforcement of rotational structures. At the same time, some rangers make requests for legitimate reasons that may include access to social services such as health and education. However, the duration of stay heightens corruption risks. This is particularly prevalent where long-term, close contact with local communities coincides with limited perceived local incentives to conserve wildlife and little oversight by management structures (GA-07, 2017[44]).

At other times, the implementation costs of functional rotation structures can delay planned mitigation measures (GA-01, 2017[82]). Wildlife management authorities are often under-resourced, at times finding themselves without the capacity to implement stated policies. Even where fully enforced, respondents questioned whether current rotation periods are sufficiently short to mitigate the corruption risks witnessed. In Kenya, for example, the current maximum posting is for three years. Certain respondents noted that this timeframe may already be too long to prevent the emergence of localised, relationship-based corruption risks (GA-02, 2017[83]). These findings points to the fact that rotation policies alone cannot be relied upon to prevent corruption from occurring in the field.

Despite rotation policies being in place for national park officers, wildlife management authorities often delegate responsibility to frontline wildlife protection positions to local officers under special arrangements. A number of respondents revealed that in some instances, such agreements do yield positive results, where local communities are engaged and derive employment from protecting wildlife through "scout" programs. However, if under-resourced or improperly managed, such institutional arrangements have created vulnerabilities to corruption. Locally based and disenfranchised officers can be much more vulnerable to corruption (see Box 3.6). From this, it is clear that rotation policies alone cannot be relied upon exclusively, and rather must be used as part of a broader anti-corruption toolkit, which also has mechanisms that ensures that both rotational and non-rotational staff are provided the adequate tools and incentives to effectively carry out their duties, while ensuring that proper accountability mechanisms are in place to prevent risks from corruption.

3.2.2. Centralisation of Wildlife Management Structures

Such local-level corruption risks relate closely to a further overarching structural issue – namely ownership of land and the wildlife that lives on it. Such arrangements are tied up with the advantages – and specifically the rent-seeking opportunities – that wildlife can bring to those who control it (Nelson, 2009[84]). Arrangements across countries can differ substantially. Many African countries have passed legislation to grant private landholders and communities rights to use wildlife on their lands, but in others wildlife remains centrally controlled national property. Zambia is an example of more centralised control: the 2015 Wildlife Act stipulates that, with specific exceptions, 'the absolute ownership of every wild animal within Zambia is vested in the President on behalf of the Republic'. While other focus countries' legislation stipulates similarly centralised custodianship, more delegated governance arrangements are also in place.

Where wildlife governance and control of wildlife user rights remain centralised, respondents highlighted significant localised corruption risks. In a highly centralised system in which communities may not feel they benefit from local resources, respondents reported higher levels of tolerance for poaching and associated corruption. In such a scenario, local communities may feel disenfranchised, perceiving little motivation to protect wildlife (FD-07, 2017[85]). This is the case particularly where poaching and trafficking are perceived to bring local benefits that outstrip those available from wildlife protection. Importantly, officers operating in such circumstances may feel less pressured to avoid engaging in corrupt activity (FD-07, 2017[85]) (NG-11, 2017[86]) (NG-13, 2017[73]) (NG-15, 2017[87]).

Box 3.4. Delegated Arrangements in Zambia

In Zambia, government-employed DNPW rangers – known as wildlife police officers – do not hold sole responsibility for frontline wildlife protection. Instead, wildlife police officers share responsibility with community scouts employed through Community Resource Boards (CRBs). These local institutional structures owe their existence to experience with Community Based Natural Resources Management strategies under the Administrative Management Design (ADMADE) for Game Management Areas in the 1980s. Following this, the 1998 Zambia Wildlife Act made specific provisions for the participation of local communities in wildlife management through CRBs.

This arrangement has inherent vulnerabilities, however. While wildlife police officers are generally better trained and subject to DNPW rotation policies, community scouts are usually community members assigned to protect wildlife *where they live*. (CLT, 2018[88]). Their status as community members can make them vulnerable to corruption attempts, of the kind that rotation policies seek to reduce. Conversely, when seeking to operate lawfully, their actions are more likely to be constrained by local hierarchies, for example where well-connected families engage in criminal or corrupt behaviours. While wildlife police officers are mandated to accompany community scouts on all patrols, respondents noted that such vulnerabilities nonetheless remain. (NG-23, 2017[53])

This situation is exacerbated by the lower and more erratic pay reportedly received by scouts relative to DNPW rangers. (GA-19, 2017[56]) (NG-23, 2017[53]) (NG-24, 2017[89]) As employees of CRBs – whose income derives from rents from recreational hunting on game management areas – community scouts' pay can fluctuate with season and demand, among other factors. Community scouts are also subject to less oversight: while under the supervisory authority of DNPW, respondents noted that a lack of resources means that their activities can go unmonitored. (NG-23, 2017[53]) (NG-25, 2017[90]). To address these issues, one respondent suggested that community scouts should be absorbed onto the DNPW payroll. However, others noted the range of problems that surround this proposal – not least the lack of resources within DNPW. In fact, many respondents noted that community scouts act as a crucial stop-gap in areas that would otherwise go unpatrolled: 31% of Zambia is covered by protected areas, with a well-placed respondent reporting an ability on the part of DNPW to sustain just over 30% of the IUCN personnel recommendation for an area this size. (GA-12, 2017[57])

These factors may also play out where legislation provides for decentralised ownership and user rights – but where these are not fully realised. In Tanzania, for example, the passage of reforms from the late 1990s sought to devolve wildlife user rights on community lands. In the Tanzanian system, Wildlife Management Areas are designated for management by communities or private actors, with monitoring and enforcement performed by village game scouts, among other actors. However, some respondents noted a perception among local people that wildlife revenues continue to bypass them (Nelson, 2009[34]) (NG-11, 2017[86]) (NG-15, 2017[87]) (IE-04, 2017[51]). This situation brings into play many of the risks mentioned above.

Indeed, across focus countries, where there is a perceived lack of local ability to capture wildlife's market value, reduced public opposition to corruption among wildlife guardians was held up as a likely result (FD-07, 2017[85]) (NG-11, 2017[86]) (NG-12, 2017[91]) (NG-13, 2017[73]). At the same time, these very factors can work powerfully against any further move toward reform. On this point, where structures remain highly centralised, Nelson has observed the 'strong incentives among some influential policy-makers and senior bureaucrats to maintain existing … governance arrangements' (Nelson, 2009[34]).

Box 3.5. A unique structural vulnerability – Tanzania and Zanzibar

An additional structural factor influencing corruption risk was cited by respondents specifically in the case of Tanzania. This revolves around differences in approach to wildlife management on the mainland, versus that in the semi-autonomous region of Zanzibar. Alongside fishing and other natural resource issues, wildlife protection is a non-union matter. As such, different legislative and institutional arrangements apply.

These differences make Zanzibar's position relative to the mainland a key facilitator of both IWT and associated corruption. In terms of legislation, Tanzania treats wildlife crime as serious crime under the UN Convention on Transnational Crime – a level of recognition that does not exist in Zanzibar. Under Tanzania's Wildlife Conservation Act 2009, the illegal selling, buying, transferring, transporting, accepting, importing or exporting of wildlife incurs a fine not less than twice the value of the trophy or a minimum of five years imprisonment (when used with the Economic and Organised Crime Act, penalties can rise to over 20 years). No such penalties are afforded by wildlife legislation in Zanzibar, where no similar Wildlife Act is in place.

Significantly, what relevant legislation exists in Zanzibar applies only to native species. Notably, it excludes most CITES-listed species, including elephants and rhinos. This loophole creates significant customs issues and, ultimately, contributes to making Zanzibar an attractive transit hub for high-value wildlife moved out from the continent.

To address this issue, Tanzania's National Ivory Action Plan mandates the preparation of CITES implementation regulations for Zanzibar. However, this process remains incomplete. The Ministry of Natural Resources and Tourism's 2017 National Ivory Action Plan Progress Report notes that CITES regulations for Zanzibar had been sent to the Attorney General of Zanzibar but returned pending a review of provisions in the Zanzibar Forest Act (MNRT , 2017[92]).

However, efforts to address the concerns of local-level actors can also be abused. A potential example lies in reports of localised embezzlement of compensation payments and diversion of funding earmarked for community projects. At the same time, more decentralised arrangements are themselves not immune to corruption risks. In Kenya, for example, a variety of local management structures exist, from local government-run reserves, to private, group and community conservancies. Here, respondents identified heightened corruption risks at the areas of interaction between local and national authorities. These were held to present themselves most clearly where autonomy from national-level structures starts and ends (NG-03, 2017[62]).

In such cases, vulnerability to corruption owes to the increased institutional "thickness" of wildlife management structures. An example of this vulnerability can be seen in the potential case of an illegal trophy seized on a local-government administered reserve. In this case, rather than directly entering KWS storage rooms, seized trophies can be kept in local storage – for subsequent collection by KWS officers (NG-03, 2017[62]). This additional layer of administration offers further opportunities for corrupt individuals to infiltrate the chain of custody – requiring exhibits to pass through additional sets of vulnerable hands. As an example, one respondent pointed to previous seizures of tusks that bore markings of non-KWS protected area storage facilities (NG-03, 2017[62]).

3.2.3. Administrative Restructuring of Wildlife Management Authorities:

A related point raised by respondents concerns the corruption risk arising where administrative structures for wildlife management are rearranged at the central level. Here, numerous respondents spoke of the instability – and corresponding opportunities for corruption – such restructuring processes can bring. Examples were cited in several countries, with some restructuring initiatives denounced as little more than 'convoluted rebranding exercises'. In other cases, respondents praised the motivation for restructuring wildlife management authorities, but expressed concerns over the corruption risks arising in the process. An example of the perceived implications of such restructuring processes is explored in Box 3.6.

Box 3.6. Institutional Restructuring in Zambia

In 2015, the Zambia Wildlife Authority (ZAWA) – then a parastatal organisation – was transformed into a government department under the Ministry of Tourism and Arts: the Department of National Parks and Wildlife. Divergent opinions were expressed around the corruption risks entailed by this shift. Several respondents cited the potential importance of Ministry control, pointing to numerous cases in which ZAWA was alleged to have dealt inadequately with corruption (GA-22, 2017[93]) (NG-21, 2017[59]) (NG-24, 2017[89]) (NG-25, 2017[90]). In 2009, for example, following a Norwegian government forensic audit related to ZAWA's support for the South Luangwa Area Management Unit, EIA alleged that the Ministry of Finance and National Planning had reported ZAWA's Director General to the Anti-Corruption Commission (EIA, 2010[33]). In a 2017 statement, Zambia's then-Minister of Tourism and Arts declared that the government had 'made the right decision to transform ZAWA into a government department' – one he declared was 'in the best interest of wildlife, the people and the country as a whole'. (Zambia Ministry of Tourism and Arts, 2017[94]) He did so citing a 26% improvement in revenue collection between 2015 and 2016, as well as an improved ability by DNPW to manage funds and ensure regular payment of salaries.

Others, however, observed the vulnerabilities associated with greater Ministry authority. They did so citing the risk that this removes autonomy and control over wildlife management from those who know the sector best (GA-18, 2017[52]). Instead, they note that removal of parastatal status places control in the hands of officials who may lack as strong an affinity for wildlife protection. Crucially, they point to the transferral of responsibility for hunting and concession tendering processes to the Ministry with the establishment of DNPW. These are processes widely alleged to be fraught with opportunities for corruption. Meanwhile, the movement of ZAWA under the Ministry of Tourism has caused concern among those who note its separation from agencies such as the Forestry Department, which sits under the Ministry of Lands, Natural Resources and Environmental Protection (GA-19, 2017[56]).

Whichever view is taken, however, a majority of respondents spoke of the corruption risks that lie in such processes of institutional transformation themselves. Here, they point to the gaps inevitably created by such reorganisations, which remain ripe for exploitation by opportunistic operators. While Ministry-level actors celebrated the move to DNPW, respondents in some parts of Zambia raised operational concerns around the restructuring process itself.[3] Notably, they cited instability surrounding the 2015 transformation as a key factor in heightened levels of poaching and associated corruption witnessed over the period. (GA-01, 2017[95]) (GA-05, 2017[43]) (GA-07, 2017[44]) (GA-12, 2017[57]) (NG-01, 2017[72]) (NG-02, 2017[96]) (NG-04, 2017[97]) (NG-18, 2017[38])

3.3. Institutional Vulnerabilities in the Criminal Justice System

Interviews conducted across all countries pointed to important vulnerabilities within the criminal justice system. Respondents identified particular vulnerabilities where cases enter the prosecution and judicial sphere. After the arrest of suspected poachers and traffickers, including potentially corrupt officials, a number of important challenges arise. Many of these challenges emerge at the very earliest stages of the criminal justice chain – with new vulnerabilities arising at each subsequent stage.

The Role of Wildlife Management Authorities in the Criminal Justice Pathway

A key set of structural risk factors raised by interviewees relates to the position of wildlife management authorities in the criminal justice pathway. In general, these authorities' ground-level responsibilities mean that they occupy only the initial stages in the criminal justice chain. In many cases, respondents described witnessing a lack of clarity among rangers on their roles at this stage of the chain as an important corruption risk. They also stressed the requirement for wildlife management authorities to pass cases on as they progress – citing the involvement of multiple agencies up the chain as a further corruption risk.

At the ground level, first, the unclear integration of rangers into the broader criminal justice chain was stressed as a vulnerability. In many cases, this was held to compound those risks embodied in rangers' distance from management structures, as examined above. In a 2017 article, Shamini Jayanathan noted a lack of adequate training for frontline protection officers on their role in the criminal justice pathway (Jayanathan, 2017[98]).

Here, the vulnerability of the system to nefarious intentions is clear. In this context, even where officers are aware of their responsibilities, inaction in exchange for bribes can be dismissed as lack of capacity (GA-03, 2017[99]) (GA-12, 2017[57]) (NG-18, 2017[38]) (NG-20, 2017[39]). At the same time, Jayanathan highlights the implications of a genuine lack of clarity on requirements to report to HQ – and on the need to be ready to write statements for the prosecution and give evidence against those charged (Jayanathan, 2017[98]). As agreed by respondents, the result can be frustration and diminishing morale over time around officers' own perceived lack of impact (GA-01, 2017[95]) (GA-09, 2017[71]). These sentiments, in turn, are cited as key factors in enhancing vulnerability to corruption.

Even where reported up from field level correctly, corruption risks were highlighted in a system in which numerous agencies are involved in pursuing a case to its conclusion. In such systems, wildlife management authorities may occupy only defined stages of the criminal justice pathway, with multiple entry points for corruption as handovers occur. In many countries, for example, the wildlife management authority is required to work closely with the police: although the former enjoys powers of arrest, the constitution may grant the police investigative authority. As cases pass between investigating authorities and on to prosecutors and magistrates, gaps in communication, prioritisation and responsibility create vulnerabilities (GA-01, 2017[95]) (GA-07, 2017[44]) (GA-12, 2017[57]) (NG-18, 2017[38]) (NG-19, 2017[100]). Across the focus countries, a lack of clarity on institutional jurisdiction was cited as a focus for corruption attempts throughout the chain. As noted by one respondent, 'Gaps and overlaps in institutional mandates make the whole criminal justice system vulnerable, from the grass-roots up' (GA-05, 2017[43]).

3.3.1. Involvement of Non-Specialised Agencies

For some, particular vulnerabilities are perceived where responsibility for combating IWT is held by agencies with broader mandates. The fear, here, is that staff of these agencies are more prone to view IWT as a trivial issue (GA-01, 2017[82]) (GA-05, 2017[43]) (GA-07, 2017[44]) (NG-18, 2017[38]) (NG-19, 2017[100]). At the local level, respondents drew attention to vulnerabilities in the police – as generalised but similarly geographically dispersed agencies. According to one, 'the police are responsible for enforcement of all laws including wildlife, with officers distributed all over the country. At the local level, they are just as vulnerable to corruption as mandated wildlife protection officers – if not more so' (GA-05, 2017[43]).

A similar vulnerability affects the military, where officers are stationed at borders or across remote areas. Here, institutional hierarchies were highlighted as a risk: in one country, respondents noted the continued sense of reverence enjoyed by the military, with many officers celebrated as national heroes (GA-12, 2017[57]) (NG-16, 2017[101]). Vulnerabilities here link to the ongoing hesitancy with which rangers and police are perceived to treat suspicious activity by military officers – who they may deem their 'superiors' in some countries. While respondents spoke of cases of military involvement (Box 3.3), they also noted a widespread failure to interdict offending officers (GA-12, 2017[57]) (NG-16, 2017[101]). Cases in which military officers declare consignments as 'security equipment' to prevent inspection were reported. At the same time, attempts to process any instances uncovered through internal mechanisms, namely court martial, were used to reduce the likelihood of serious consequences.

A key fear among some respondents is that such non-wildlife focused agencies view IWT as a minor issue. In such cases, officers can more easily be bribed to release suspects, lose evidence post-arrest, tamper with charge sheets, ensure evidence is inadmissible by giving conflicting statements, or otherwise obstruct an investigation. Such concerns apply similarly further up the criminal justice chain: in the case of prosecution and judicial services, officers have been known to falsify evidence, delay hearings or in myriad other ways jeopardise a case (GA-09, 2017[71]) (GA-20, 2017[102]) (NG-01, 2017[72]) (NG-02, 2017[96]) (NG-04, 2017[97]) (NG-21, 2017[59]). For wildlife management authorities looking to operate effectively, such corruption risks are destructive. Most damagingly, they can result in failure to achieve criminal justice outcomes, even where wildlife management officers correctly draft statements and recommend charges, contact the prosecution authority, and take and exhibit photos in line with legal requirements.

Where a full evidential file does not result in conviction, the knock-on impact on honest wildlife management officers can be highly negative. For these officers, such incidents, repeated over time, can reduce both willingness to risk their lives on the frontline – and inclination to resist corruption attempts in anticipation of a larger law-enforcement impact (GA-12, 2017[57]) (NG-12, 2017[91]) (NG-19, 2017[100]) (NG-24, 2017[89]). In numerous interviews, respondents cited the poor and irregular pay received by rangers – contrasting this with the much larger rewards on offer to 'look the other way' (GA-05, 2017[43]) (GA-06, 2017[103]) (GA-11, 2017[104]) (GA-13, 2017[45]) (IO-02, 2017[42]) (NG-21, 2017[59]). Just as frequently, however, they cited lack of morale as influencing vulnerability – and the impact on morale of negative outcomes up the chain. One interviewee described wildlife officers as 'victims of circumstances, who depend on other agencies for positive outcomes. Rangers regularly hand poachers over to the police, who then simply set them free' (GA-06, 2017[103]).

3.3.2. Institutional Gaps during Prosecution and Sentencing

Respondents identified a range of vulnerabilities where cases enter the prosecution and judicial sphere. As noted by Jayanathan in a 2016 analysis, across African range states 'training and sensitisation of prosecutors and judges rarely … tackles the issue of corruption within the context of a criminal trial' (Jayanathan, 2017[98]). Of course, corruption can be challenging to differentiate from lack of competence: as one interviewee observed, 'which one conceals the other is far from apparent' (NG-04, 2017[97]). However, the results in many cases are striking. In Kenya, respondents cited a

2014 survey of 743 cases of wildlife crime from 2008 to 2013, in which as many as 70% of case files were reported 'missing' or misplaced by the courts (Kahumbu et al., 2014[26]). Of the 224 offenders found guilty of wildlife crimes, only 8 (a mere 4%) went to jail.

The survey, as well as numerous respondents, concludes that 'wildlife related crime … is treated as a misdemeanour or petty crime and is "mismanaged" within the Kenyan court systems' (Kahumbu et al., 2014[26]). Notably, interviewees recounted witnessing a significant range of prosecutorial and judicial 'irregularities' – extending beyond those described in the published literature. Among the most common issues cited were loss of or tampering with case files; loss of or tampering with exhibits and other evidence; and replacement of exhibits with smaller items. In Kenya, respondents spoke of wildlife exhibits whittled down between arrest and trial – replaced again and again by ever-smaller replacements. 'When a case starts, there is typically a huge amount of ivory; when it ends, a tiny amount remains', observed one (NG-01, 2017[72]). In other cases, magistrates may see the same piece of ivory again and again – being substituted in and out. In still other cases, exhibits have been known to disappear altogether, as examined in more detail below.

Further corrupt actions cited by respondents included interference with witnesses; bribing of magistrates by the accused to grant bail; and bribing of magistrates to give a particular sentence. Here, the role of an accused's defence lawyer was emphasised: this individual was described repeatedly as prone to run corrupt negotiations on behalf of the accused (GA-09, 2017[71]) (GA-17-2017, 2017[63]). The issuance of direct threats to prosecutors or magistrates, or their families, was also cited as a key risk (NG-17, 2017[105]). Similar threats were said to be used against witnesses and officers – to prevent a case proceeding as it should.

A number of these risks are referenced by Kahumbu et al. in their 2014 survey of IWT cases in Kenya. Although not able to disaggregate incompetence from corruption, a number of indicators of corruption are referenced. For example, the authors cite instances where trophies 'disappeared' from exhibit rooms, as well as cases in which exhibits had been 'recycled' (Kahumbu et al., 2014[26]). Meanwhile, despite repeated media reports of corruption linked to IWT, strikingly, the authors note that 'no single case against a government officer could be found in the court records'.

In a key observation, Kahumbu et al. link poor charging decisions and a failure to apply ancillary orders such as forfeiture to particular institutional arrangements for processing IWT cases. In particular, the report – and a number of respondents – links poor outcomes to the fact that IWT offences were then charged and disposed of by police prosecutors, and were not always reported to KWS or the Office of the Director of Public Prosecutions (ODPP). The report notes that this situation could owe to a possible 'lack of awareness by police prosecutors' (Kahumbu et al., 2014[26]). However, a number of interviewees – in Kenya and elsewhere – cited corruption explicitly as a factor where non-specialised officers assume such duties, independent of mandated wildlife management authorities (GA-12, 2017[57]) (GA-14, 2017[106]).

In Kenya, the situation has since changed with the passage of the 2013 Wildlife Conservation and Management Act (WCMA). This grants prosecutorial powers to ODPP and KWS prosecutors – an act accompanied by the establishment of a wildlife crime unit in the ODPP, and the operationalisation of a prosecution unit in KWS[4]. At the same time, in an effort to improve both the strength and deterrent impact of sentences handed down, the WCMA has enhanced penalties for wildlife offenders. In particular, section 92 provides sentences of life imprisonment and/or minimum fines of 20 million Kenyan shillings (around $200,000) for crimes against endangered species.

On the latter point, however, some respondents noted that the adoption of high minimum sentences may have perverse impacts. It is possible, they observe, that such changes can in fact enhance incentives for corruption, in some cases (NG-04, 2017[97]). In Kenya, in contrast to the small fines and short jail time handed out prior to 2013, the WCMA has changed the risk-reward calculus of poachers and traffickers. Prior to 2013, Kahumbu et al. noted that 'leniency in the majority of sentencing encourages suspects to plead guilty at first appearance, [or to] change their plea to guilty after first appearance' (Kahumbu et al., 2014[26]). Since 2013, however, respondents pointed to an increasing propensity to plead 'not guilty', while resorting to corruption to influence proceedings (NG-04, 2017[97]) (NG-08, 2017[107]). With few remaining options to pay small fines, legislative reform of this kind – whilst a clear statement of intent – may thus inadvertently increase corruption risk.

3.3.3. Vulnerabilities around 'Case Drift'

Stronger penalties can also do little to prevent the irregularities discussed above. Where these irregularities amass, they can result in substantial 'case drift' – with cases pending, at times, over periods extending years. In some cases, drift was blamed on lack of capacity and existing chronic delays in court systems (GA-01, 2017[82]) (GA-14, 2017[106]) (NG-04, 2017[97]) (NG-13, 2017[73]). Respondents nevertheless observed its implications for corruption risk. Here, they noted the greater timeframe this allows a defendant to establish who to corrupt and how. As observed by one respondent, 'a key facilitator of corruption is the significant amount of time that can pass from time of arrest to sentencing – providing ample time for corrupt negotiations to take place' (NG-14, 2017[108]).

In other cases, respondents spoke of the pursuit of 'case drift' as a deliberate strategy to weaken and ultimately destroy a case. This is achieved by ensuring exhibits are lost and witnesses are unavailable. Those orchestrating the situation are aware of the impact of persistent adjournments on even the best investigations and prosecutions (GA-01, 2017[82]) (GA-14, 2017[106]) (NG-04, 2017[97]). This situation speaks to a concept described in a report produced for the Kenya Forestry Service, namely that of 'time as a resource that can be corrupted' (KFS, 2010[109]). The report described how 'the cumulative cost of … [some] behavior may even transcend direct forms of corruption such as monetary bribes'.

In some cases, such derailments can ensure that the accused is never convicted. Even where convicted, meanwhile, corrupt targeting of magistrates can ensure that weak sentences are handed down. Here, respondents cited vulnerabilities to corruption in a lack of awareness among many magistrates of the severity and broader societal impact of many IWT issues (GA-13, 2017[45]) (NG-04, 2017[97]) (NG-12, 2017[91]) (NG-24, 2017[89]) (NG-25, 2017[90]). Where magistrates view wildlife crime as an issue of limited importance, many respondents noted, corruption attempts become less difficult to accept.

This vulnerability is said to be enhanced by the lack of external involvement in sentencing decisions. Respondents from one government administration and several NGOs noted that the significant discretion typically enjoyed by magistrates makes corruption attempts easy to accept and fulfil (GA-09, 2017[71]) (NG-17, 2017[105]) (NG-23, 2017[53]) (NG-24, 2017[89]). Across some focus countries, meanwhile, an inability to appeal the handing down of inadequate sentences was held to make it difficult to challenge corruption at judicial level. In Tanzania and Uganda, for example, prosecutors do not have the right to appeal such decisions; in Kenya, this power exists, but has not yet been used (NG-04, 2017[97]). Finally, in all countries, respondents spoke of the potential role of corruption post-conviction, with questionable appeals underway in a number of cases (GA-09, 2017[71]) (NG-02, 2017[96]) (NG-05, 2017[110]).

References

CLT (2018), *Conservation Lake Tanganyika: Supporting Field Rangers*, http://conservationtanganyika.org/projects/village-scout-unit/.

EIA (2010), *Open Season: The Burgeoning Illegal Ivory Trade in Tanzania and Zambia*, http://dx.doi.org/\.

EIA (2016), *Time for Action: End the Criminality and Corruption Fuelling Wildlife Crime*.

FD-02 (2017), "REPRESENTATIVES OF FOREIGN DELEGATION 3, 4: Governance and Multilateral Affairs advisors at Foreign Delegation, in Person interview, Friday 8 September, 2017".

FD-03 (2017), "REPRESENTATIVES OF FOREIGN DELEGATION 5, 6: Defense and Trade Advisors at Foreign Delegation, in person interview, Monday 4 September, 2017".

FD-07 (2017), "REPRESENTATIVES OF FOREIGN DELEGATION 11, 12: Deputy Head and Policy Advisors of Foreign Delegation, Tuesday 12 December, 2017".

GA-01 (2017), "REPRESENTATIVES OF GOVERNMENT AGENCY 1, 2, 3, 4: In person interview, Thursday 7 September".

GA-01 (2017), "REPRESENTATIVES OF GOVERNMENT AGENCY 1, 2, 3, 4: In person interview, Thursday 7 September,".

GA-02 (2017), "REPRESENTATIVE OF GOVERNMENT AGENCY 5: In Person interview Thursday 7 September, BY PHONE".

GA-03 (2017), "REPRESENTATIVE OF GOVERNMENT AGENCY 6: In person interview, Friday 8 September, 2017".

GA-05 (2017), "REPRESENTATIVE OF GOVERNMENT AGENCY 8: In person interview, Wednesday 13 December 2017".

GA-07 (2017), "REPRESENTATIVES OF GOVERNMENT AGENCY 10, 11: In person interview, Friday 15 December 2017".

GA-09 (2017), "REPRESENTATIVES OF GOVERNMENT AGENCY 14, 15: In person Interview, Friday 15 December 2017".

GA-12 (2017), "REPRESENTATIVES OF GOVERNMENT AGENCY 20, 21: In person interview, Tuesday 5 September 2017".

GA-16((n.d.)), "REPRESENTATIVE OF GOVERNMENT AGENCY 34: Monday 11 December 2017", *2017*.

GA-18 (2017), "REPRESENTATIVES OF GOVERNMENT AGENCY 27, 27, 28, 29: In person interview, Tuesday 12 December 2017".

GA-19 (2017), "REPRESENTATIVE OF GOVERNMENT AGENCY 30: In person interview, Tuesday 12 December 2017".

GA-22 (2017), "REPRESENTATIVE OF GOVERNMENT AGENCY 34: Phone interview Friday 26 January 2017".

IE-01 (2017), "INDEPENDENT EXPERT 1: In person interview Friday 8 September,".

IE-04 (2017), "INDEPENDENT EXPERT 4: In person interview, Tuesday 5 September 2017".

Jayanathan, S. (2017), "Frontline Protection and the Rule of Law – Missing a Link?", *Justice for Wildlife blog* December, http://dx.doi.org/Frontline Protection and the Rule of Law – Missing a Link?', Justice for Wildlife blog, 14 December 2017, https://justiceforwildlife.com/frontline-protection-rule-law-missing-link/.

Jayanathan, S. (2016), *Stopping Poaching and Wildlife Trafficking through Strengthened Laws and Improved Application. Phase I: An Analysis of Criminal Justice Interventions across African Ranges States and Proposals for Action.*

KWS (2018), *Kenya Wildlife Service, 'About Us'*, http://www.kws.go.ke/about-us/about-us.

KWS (2017), "Review of KWS Standing Orders and Disciplinary Code", http://www.kws.go.ke/content/review-kws-standing-orders-and-disciplinary-code.

KWS (2015), "Kenya Wildlife Service: Annual Report 2015".

MNRT (2017), "CITES National Ivory Action Plan Progress Report. Reporting period: 1st January 2017 – 31st December 2017'", *Tanzania Ministry of Natural Resources and Tourism.*

Nelson, F. (2009), "Reforming Wildlife Governance in East and Southern Africa: The Role of Corruption", *U4 Brief* 12.

Nelson, F. (2009), "Reforming Wildlife Governance in East and Southern Africa: The Role of Corruption'", *U4 Brief*, Vol. 12.

NG-01 (2017), "REPRESENTATIVE OF WILDLIFE NGO 1: In person Interview, Thursday 7 September,".

NG-02 (2017), "REPRESENTATIVE OF NGO 2: In person interview, Thursday 7 September,".

NG-03 (2017), "REPRESENTATIVE OF NGO 3: in person interview, Friday 8 September, 2017".

NG-04 (2017), "REPRESENTATIVE OF NGO 4: In person interview, Friday 8 September, 2017".

NG-11 (2017), "REPRESENTATIVE OF NGO 10: In person interview, Thursday 14 December 2017".

NG-12 (2017), "REPRESENTATIVE OF NGO 11: In person interview, 14 December 2017".

NG-13 (2017), "REPRESENTATIVE OF NGO 12: In person interview, 14".

NG-15 (2017), "REPRESENTATIVE OF NGO 15: In person interview, Thursday 14 December 2017".

NG-18 (2017), "REPRESENTATIVE OF NGO 21: In person interview, Tuesday 5 September,".

NG-20 (2017), "REPRESENTATIVE OF NGO 23: In person interview, Wednesday 6 September 2017".

NG-21 (2017), "REPRESENTATIVES OF NGO 24, 25: In person interview, Monday 11 December 2017".

NG-23 (2017), "REPRESENTATIVES OF NGO 27, 28: In person interview, Tuesday 12 December 2017".

NG-24 (2017), "REPRESENTATIVE OF NGO 29, 30: Skype interview, 15 December 2017".

NG-25 (2017), "REPRESENTATIVE OF NGO 31: Skype interview, Wednesday 20 December, 2017".

URT (2017), *United Republic of Tanzania (URT) Natural Resources and Tourism Report: 'CITES National Ivory Action Plan Progress Report. Reporting period: 1st January 2017 – 31st December 2017'.*.

UWA((n.d.)), *Uganda Wildlife Authority, 'About Us'*, http://www.ugandawildlife.org/about-uganda-master/uganda-wildlife-authority.

Zambia Ministry of Tourism and Arts (2017), *Statement by Hon. Charles R. Banda, MP, Minister of Tourism and Arts, on the Transformation of Zambia Wildlife Authority into the Department of Parks and Wildlife, 27 June 2017.*

Notes

[1] The 2017 OECD Recommendations provide a detailed "comprehensive policy framework for reinforcing integrity and managing ethics in the public sector through a whole-of-government and whole-of-society approach". In order achieve this culture of public integrity; anti-corruption agencies must have the responsibility to conduct awareness raising, prevention, investigation and enforcement of corruption in the public sector.

[2] In Kenya, a significant amount of wildlife lives outside gazetted parks and reserves, and as such KWS also manages 125 field stations outside protected areas (KWS, 2018[77]).

[3] It should be noted that many of the same concerns were expressed around the ongoing restructuring of wildlife management arrangements in Tanzania.

[4] Section 107 of the WCMA provides for powers of prosecution, including for delegated powers of prosecution to be afforded to KWS officers. Part XIII of the same Act provides for powers of investigation, arrest and enforcement to be afforded to authorised KWS officers. (KWS, 2015[170])

4. IWT and Corruption Risks: Supply-Chain Factors

This chapter provides a supply-chain perspective on corruption, focusing on corruption risks along the source and transit points of illegal wildlife products. The report highlights where the corruption risks are highest and what regional variations exist across focus countries that enable such risks.

'Corruption is distributed along the length of the chain a wildlife product follows, from park to lorry, to container, to ship. The nature of corruption along the chain depends on the value of the cargo and the amount of profit to be made' (GA-01, 2017[82]).

In addition to the structural factors covered in Chapter 3, a second broad set of factors were held to affect corruption risks around IWT across the focus countries. These link to the particular position each country occupies within the global IWT supply chain.

All four focus countries act as source and transit countries for illegal wildlife products, with a number of activities taking place at each stage. Supply chain movements range broadly from illegal sourcing of a wildlife product to localised transit and consolidation, prior to export and international transit towards destination states.

Variations in the extent of these activities across each focus country affect the form and dynamics of corruption risks witnessed. First, the chapter examines the position of each country in the broader IWT chain and the corresponding corruption risks witnessed across them. Second, it examines variations in the supply chain for different species present in the focus countries – and their corresponding impact on corruption risk.

4.1. Regional Variation of Supply-Chain Factors

A crucial point that remains under-acknowledged in the published literature is the extent to which corruption risks vary by country. This variation owes to the fact that countries in the same region occupy – at times substantially – different positions in the broader IWT supply chain. Of course, some corruption risks are common to multiple countries, including at the source and transit stages. However, semi-structured interviews revealed a number of differences across the focus countries in the precise profile of corruption risks cited.

Kenya, Tanzania, Uganda and Zambia share the distinction of acting as source and transit countries in the broader IWT supply chain. However, a closer look at each country reveals key differences in the extent of their roles in sourcing and transit processes, as follows.

4.1.1. Uganda

Uganda acts predominantly as a transit point for high-value wildlife products, such as ivory and rhino horn. Following the dramatic losses witnessed in the 1960s and 1970s, the country's elephant population remains low but stable at around 5,000 animals, with only a smaller number of well-guarded rhinos based at a rhino breeding and rehabilitation facility (Great Elephant Census, 2015[111]). Instead, poaching is largely restricted to bush meat, pangolin and hippo teeth. As one interviewee expressed, 'Uganda is mainly a transit hub for ivory and rhino horn – corruption here is a bigger problem when it comes to facilitating transport activity, than when it comes to facilitating poaching itself' (GA-10, 2017[41]).

4.1.2. Kenya

In Kenya, respondents emphasised similarly that corruption facilitating transit activity was likely to be more significant than that facilitating poaching itself. (GA-01, 2017[82]) (NG-01, 2017[72]) (NG-07, 2017[112]) Of relevance here is the extent to which the dominant IWT threat facing the country has shifted over time. In the early years of this decade, the country experienced a dramatic surge in poaching, peaking in 2012-2013. In these two years, Kenya lost more elephants and rhinos than at any time in the past two decades. (Vaughan, 2016[113]) Thanks to concerted law enforcement action against illegal killing, however, this poaching surge has since waned.

Strikingly, from 384 elephants poached in 2012, levels of illegal killing dropped to 302 in 2013, 164 in 2014, 96 in 2015 to 86 in 2016, according to KWS figures (Koech, 2017[114]). From 59 rhinos poached in 2013, levels of illegal killing have similarly dropped to 35 killed in 2014 and 11 in 2015 (Koech, 2017[114]). This has occurred despite continued, regular seizures of large (over 500 kg) ivory consignments that have transited the Kenyan port of Mombasa. However, such seizures have rarely led to the disruption of networks of handlers and corrupt officials operating within the Kenyan context. As such, Kenya continues to act as a key transit country, even as its role as a source country has diminished. With a major international shipping port and significant international airports, Kenya remains a significant transit hub for IWT products.

4.1.3. Tanzania

Tanzania continues to play a crucial role as both a source and a transit country. Government figures released in 2015 highlighted the country's role at the epicentre of Africa's poaching crisis. These indicated a drop in the country's elephant population of 60% in just five years, from 109,051 in 2009 to just 43,330 in 2014 (CITES, 2017[9]) (Mathiesen, 2015[115]). DNA testing by researchers at Washington State University singled out the Selous/Niassa ecosystem in southeast Tanzania/northern Mozambique as the source of 86–93% of savannah elephant ivory found in large seizures from 2006 to 2014 (Wasser et al., 2015[116]).

Since then, however, poaching levels appear to have decreased. Figures presented by the Ministry of Natural Resources and Tourism show a significant drop in Proportion of Illegally Killed Elephant (PIKE) values (which measure illegally killed carcasses as a proportion of total carcasses). Notably, data for the period 2015–16 show a significant drop in PIKE values in Ruaha-Rungwa, where the PIKE value dropped by 37%; and in Selous-Mikumi, where it dropped by 35% (MNRT , 2017[92]) (CITES, 2017[9]). However, these declines have taken place against a high baseline, with poaching levels nonetheless remaining higher than in many other locations. This owes to Tanzania's significant remaining, vulnerable elephant populations, which continue to make the country a key target. As noted by CITES, Tanzania remains the region's elephant population stronghold, with an estimated 50,433 elephants in the country in 2015 (CITES, 2017[9]). Meanwhile, with several major international port installations and international airports, Tanzania remains a departure point for large volumes of IWT products.

4.1.4. Zambia

For its part, Zambia plays both source and transit roles in the global IWT supply chain. Notably, its significant elephant populations – just over 21,750 in 2015 – ensure that the country remains a focus for high-value poaching activity (Republic of Zambia, 2015[117]). Although the 2015 Great Elephant Census revealed stable populations overall, it showed declines in Lower Zambezi and 'catastrophic declines' in Sioma Ngwezi National Park (Great Elephant Census, 2016[118]). Meanwhile, ivory – as well as pangolin and other wildlife – sourced in the country is transported along diverse routes for export to East and Southeast Asia. While playing a significant transit role, however, the landlocked country does not possess the large-scale port facilities of Kenya or Tanzania. As such, transit and export activity here often takes a different form – oriented instead towards vehicular transit across land borders and international airports.

4.2. Corruption Risks at Sourcing and Local Transit Level

The differing extent and nature of the source and transit roles the four countries play is a crucial determiner of the corruption risks seen in each. This owes to the very different forms of corruption required in relation to the illegal sourcing of wildlife products, relative to consolidation and large-scale transit of high-value, high-stakes consignments. In relation to illegal sourcing, respondents noted that corruption tends to be low-level – involving relatively small amounts of money paid to field level officials (GA-04, 2017[37]) (NG-12, 2017[91]) (NG-19, 2017[100]) (NG-21, 2017[59]). If a situation arises where poachers are caught, corruption appears to assume an ad-hoc form, with bribes paid only if perpetrators are stopped and searched. A brief look at the most prevalent risks cited at each level is useful to determine the corruption profiles likely faced by each country under consideration.

4.2.1. Direct Facilitation of Poaching

At poaching level, respondents cited corruption risks as taking a range of forms. Notably, interviews revealed a substantially broader range of potential manifestations than those covered in the published literature. In particular, interviewees implicated wildlife officers in engaging directly in poaching, in handing out intelligence on patrol patterns, and in failing to patrol or respond to poaching incidents (GA-03, 2017[99]) (GA-07, 2017[44]) (GA-13, 2017[45]) (GA-20, 2017[102]) (NG-23, 2017[53]) (NG-24, 2017[89]). Similar risks exist where officials divulge information on wildlife positions – in many cases, rangers must record the coordinates of rhino locations, which can be handed to poachers for bribes.

Here, differences between target species come into play. Low-value species, for example, are not heavily guarded and may require little facilitation to poach. At this level, bribes are declared by respondents to be paid only if intercepted (GA-04, 2017[37]) (GA-06, 2017[103]) (NG-19, 2017[100]).

For higher-value species, protection arrangements are typically more sophisticated. The most extreme example concerns rhinos – whose horn is often said to be worth more per kilo than cocaine or gold (Wolpert, 2015[119]). As such, rhino populations in Kenya, for example, are carefully monitored and guarded. Here, corruption was said to become a more necessary strategy – not only in preventing interception, but in gaining access to the animals in the first instance. According to one respondent, 'almost every rhino poached in Kenya is an inside job' (IE-02-2017, 2017[120]).

4.2.2. Loaning of Weapons and Ammunition

Other actions, such as the loaning of weapons and ammunition to poachers are common. In Tanzania, for example, a recent investigatory report implicated rangers in the Ruaha National Parks in the provision of ammunition to poachers. Reporters claim to have uncovered 'evidence of collusion' between rangers and the poachers they were supposed to be stopping (Deutsche Welle, 2017[121]). The claims lay in scientific analysis of Great Elephant Census surveys, showing clusters of carcasses only 500 metres from ranger posts. The report notes that 'there are hotspots around 2 or 3 of the ranger posts and it's hard to explain those except in relation to the ranger posts'. Accompanying testimony from a ranger alleges internal facilitation of poaching activity mainly through the loaning of ammunition to poachers.

Other armed officers, such as police and military are also alleged to provide weapons and ammunition to poachers (FD-04, 2017[122]) (FD-06, 2017:[123]) (NG-17, 2017[105]). Military officials often have access to larger stockpiles of ammunition in comparison to rangers. In one case, poachers were reported to have obtained munitions from a specific military barracks and, in turn, shared their earnings with the corrupt officers involved (NG-17, 2017[105]). However, the distinction between military officers and rangers may be hard to make in some instances[1].

4.2.3. Acceptance of Bribes to Release Poachers

If a situation arises whereby a poacher or person implicated along the IWT trade chain is apprehended, bribes or other favours may be exchanged to secure the release of a suspect. In the field, wildlife protection officers are vulnerable to external pressure to release individuals from custody. However, a number of other ground-level agencies – beyond wildlife management authorities are held to be implicated as well. (GA-02, 2017[83]) (GA-05, 2017[43]) (GA-12, 2017[57]) (IE-03, 2017[124]) (NG-14, 2017[108]). Arresting officers can be rangers, but also police or army officers, stationed at checkpoints in the vicinity. In Uganda, where poaching – predominantly of lower-value species – often brings in only modest sums, relatively small amounts of money can secure release of suspects. Respondents also suggested that these sums could be negotiated by community leaders looking to protect constituents. At other times, pressure may be applied from within central agencies; according to one respondent, 'there is often central-level pressure on police and wildlife authority staff to "let things move" at a park level' (GA-12, 2017[57]).

This point links to the relevance of strong institutional hierarchies. In many of the focus countries, a strong sense of hierarchy exists; according to one interviewee, 'it is very difficult for an officer to question his superiors' (NG-18, 2017[38]). This speaks to an important set of factors around workplace intimidation and even coercion. So-called 'orders given from above' indicate a structural nuance to the conventional understanding of bribery and corruption as a transactional arrangement between one corrupt agent and another. (GA-09, 2017[71]) (GA-12, 2017[57]) (GA-20, 2017[102]) (NG-18, 2017[38]) (NG-19, 2017[100]). Respondents quoted commonly heard phrases such as 'let this one go' – sent down as instructions from the higher levels. At the same time, respondents noted that corrupt orders might be excused as 'having come from even further up'. In implying that this is the case, individuals can exonerate themselves to those below as simply the messenger for a higher-level corrupt request.

4.2.4. Stockpile Theft

As noted, such corruption risks were described as affecting officers from a diversity of ground-level agencies. Other risks were reported similarly to affect a range of agencies, most notably involvement in the theft of seized exhibits from wildlife management authority and police store rooms. Instances of corruption at strong rooms were cited across the focus countries – backed up at times by media coverage.

In some cases, the amounts can be highly significant. In Uganda, the discovery of the theft of 1.35 tons of ivory from UWA strong rooms in November 2014 provides a telling example. A similar example in Zambia saw reports in June 2012 of the disappearance of an estimated 3 tons of ivory (Box 4.1). In December 2014, meanwhile, the theft of more than 30 pieces of ivory tusk from a ZAWA storeroom in Livingstone was uncovered (Box 4.1).

Box 4.1. Ivory thefts from Zambia stores

In June 2012, ZAWA announced that three tons of ivory had been stolen from its holding office in Chilanga, Lusaka. Two game scouts were apprehended in connection with the incident. The then-director general of ZAWA reportedly noted that the discovery was made during a routine stock-take, and that tampering with air ventilators and burglar bars was evident (Zambia Reports, 2012[125]).

Conservationists pointed to the scale of the theft, saying that it could only have occurred as a result of high-level corruption. Concerns were also raised at inconsistencies between statements from ZAWA and those from the police. The theft of the 'missing ivory' was subsequently alleged to be linked to top ruling-party officials engaged in fundraising for by-elections in Livingstone, Chama North and Muchinga constituencies (Zambian Watchdog, 2012[126]).

In a further incident in December 2014, more than 30 pieces of ivory tusk were stolen from a ZAWA storeroom in Livingstone (Namaiko, 2014[127]). A Southern Province Police Chief confirmed that the pieces of ivory had been exhibits for a case then in court. Eight of the ten individuals investigated were arrested, including three ZAWA officers.

Such opportunities arise amid poor security and management of stockpiles in a number of locations. Here, respondents described stockpiles in distant parks and police stations as particularly vulnerable, with inventories less consistently conducted and maintained. In many such cases, wildlife management authority headquarters can reportedly be unaware of the precise volumes in stock in each location. As noted by one respondent, the practice of rotating staff involved in stockpile management and inventory processes presents further vulnerabilities in this regard (NG-17, 2017[105]).

These corruption risks are held to affect different countries – and locations within them – differently. In particular, risks were said to vary in line with the specific stockpile management policies in place in each case. In Kenya, notably, the 2016 burn of 105 tonnes of ivory – the country's entire holdings and an estimated 5% of global stock – is said to have reduced the risks linked to stockpile theft (Smith, 2016[128]). In other focus countries, however, the risk is held to remain high – with different levels of stockpile security and inventory support in place in each case.

As noted, the extent of such source-level risks in each country varies. It does so in line with the extent of the poaching witnessed – relative to other IWT threats. Indeed, while highly relevant in a number of focus countries, in countries such as Uganda interviewees cited corruption at transit level as presenting the greater issue. The following sub-section will consider the differential corruption risks described by respondents at this level.

4.3. Corruption Risks at National and International Transit Level

A common separation point was described by respondents between the corruption risks seen at sourcing level versus those seen at transit level for products such as ivory. This separation point was observed to be the point of consolidation of a larger illegal wildlife shipment. From this point, corruption was described as assuming a range of diverse forms to those seen at lower levels. Notably, from this point on, the more organised, pervasive and complex nature of the corruption encountered was consistently brought out by respondents.

4.3.1. Pre-emptive versus ad-hoc corruption

This greater complexity owes to the higher value assumed by illegal wildlife products once amassed into a single consignment. Whether ivory or pangolin scales, from this point, respondents noted the altered risk calculus of the traffickers involved. Above all, a difference appears to emerge in the extent to which bribery to secure safe passage is pre-planned and pre-meditated, versus ad hoc, based on whether or not interdiction occurs. Here, a distinction was made between pre-interception, 'pre-emptive' corruption to gain clear passage in advance – and ad-hoc, post-interception corruption to secure release (GA-04, 2017[37]) (GA-07, 2017[44]) (GA-14, 2017[106]) (NG-12, 2017[91]) (NG-19, 2017[100]).

Of course, some source- and local transit-level corruption risks see officers engaged directly in poaching, or approached proactively, in advance, to gain access to animals. However, at this lower level, bribery to secure safe passage of poached wildlife products was cited generally as happening on a needs-only basis. According to one respondent, 'at the pre-consolidation level, particularly between field and warehouse, pre-emptive bribery to secure safe passage is not common. To reduce costs, it is employed only where necessary – upon interception or arrest' (GA-10, 2017[41]). As such, corruption appears to be treated as a business cost – to be kept to a minimum and utilised only when required. As a result, corrupt arrangements are generally described as ad hoc – with little effort made to maintain long-term ties over time.

This modus operandi is held to change post-consolidation. From this point in the chain, corruption is more likely to be used pre-emptively, to ensure consignments clear passage. As noted by one respondent, from storage point on, 'corrupt officers are likely to be maintained in anticipation of need, rather than employed on an ad hoc basis'. In a 2017 EIA report, this was described as 'owning the road' – a process involving the establishment of 'a safe route with trusted accomplices operating along the way' (EIA, 2017[129]).

The light shone on this process by EIA is important. 'If the route is broken', the report notes, 'operations have to be disrupted as new allegiances are formed'. Tellingly, the report describes the confidence of a syndicate of Tanzanian and Mozambican suppliers operating out of the northern Mozambican port of Pemba in the extent of their 'ownership of the road'. Here, particular arrangements were made around a 2016 ivory consignment bound for another group in Shuidong, China, including an agreement that 'should the shipment be seized, the Mozambican and Tanzanian suppliers would compensate the Shuidong group for the full cost of the container' (EIA, 2017[129]).

4.3.2. The role of chokepoints

Such pre-emptive arrangements become particularly crucial where a consignment must transit key transport hubs. Described by respondents as 'chokepoints', it is here that corrupt facilitation is held to become most vital. Such chokepoints comprise the points at which products are channelled through key pathways, whether official border crossings, ports or airports. In a May 2015 report, C4ADS speak of both 'maritime chokepoints' and 'airborne chokepoints' along trafficking routes (Miller et al., 2015[130]). Their existence owes to the fact that wildlife trafficking networks typically do not maintain their own parallel supply chains. Instead, they use the established transportation infrastructure in place to process legitimate global trade.

Particularly vital chokepoints exist where consignments enter international transportation channels. Here, respondents cited key vulnerabilities to corruption – describing international ports and airports as points where corrupt ties grow most critical. Of relevance here are the more stringent controls in place on merchandise passing through to other markets. However, also of relevance is the greater institutional complexity characteristic of these crucial nodes in the chain.

Indeed, in many cases, multi-agency teams are deployed at wildlife trafficking chokepoints. In Tanzania, for example, Joint Port Control Units exist at Dar es Salaam port, bringing together the Tanzania Police Force, Tanzania Ports Authority, Tanzania Revenue Authority, Wildlife Division and Tanzania Forest Service Agency, which are trained in profiling techniques. At Kampala's customs dry port, similar joint units bring together the Uganda Police Force, Uganda Revenue Authority and Uganda Wildlife Authority. In Mombasa, a further Joint Port Control Unit brings together the Kenya Police Service, Kenya Wildlife Service, Kenya Forest Service, Kenya Ports Authority and Kenya Revenue Authority.

As a result, depending on the specific arrangements in place, corruption attempts must become more sophisticated. As such, in several focus countries, respondents spoke of a 'web of official complicity' at key chokepoints. One observed: 'corruption is run through networks', involving the construction of a web of corrupt relationships across agencies (GA-12, 2017[57]). The greater sophistication of corrupt networks at this level means that some may facilitate multiple crimes at once – whether involving the movement of ivory, drugs or other illicit commodities. According to another respondent, 'corruption networks are highly interwoven' – with officers from multiple agencies collaborating, often across crime types, to achieve a desired end (NG-20, 2017[39]).

4.3.3. The role of private-sector corruption

The complexity of corruption at this stage only increases with the involvement of private-sector actors. Here, numerous respondents noted the critical role of private-sector corruption in facilitating the passage of multi-ton consignments. This owes again to the legitimate transportation infrastructure typically employed by wildlife traffickers. As described in a recent C4ADS report, to minimise chances of interception, traffickers seek to 'nest' their illicit activities within licit business and transportation enterprises (Miller et al., 2015[130]).

Here, a corruption risk lies in attempts to obscure beneficial ownership and sources of contraband through the establishment of shell organisations. Through this practice, trafficking networks look to disguise illicit activities as legitimate. The process of registering such companies does not always involve corruption. In many cases, weak corporate transparency standards and company incorporation requirements in focus countries mitigate the need. For example, a 2012 study suggested that Kenya might rank first globally in terms of ease of setting up a company without identifying documents. (Findley et al., 2012[131]) In other cases, however, respondents spoke of encountering private-sector collusion in the registration of companies used to hide wildlife trafficking activity.

Once front companies have been set up, respondents spoke of other corruption risks facing private-sector actors. Here, many cited risks around the work of clearing and forwarding, logistics and ground handling service providers. Others described vulnerabilities around container-, shipping- and trucking-leasing companies – as well as warehousing companies – in focus countries. According to one respondent, 'in terms of private sector corruption, the number one problem sits with clearing and forwarding companies' (NG-17, 2017[105]). Reinforcing this, C4ADS note that 'transportation and financial services companies that clear transactions between Africa and East Asia face a particularly high risk of exposure' (Miller et al., 2015[130]).

With responsibilities for customs clearance, cargo handling, port storage and logistics, such companies clearly present unique corruption opportunities. Exploiting their proximity to the transit process, interviewees spoke of longstanding corrupt ties between traffickers and corrupt staff of such companies – whether operational or higher level officers. Approaches to building these relationships can vary: in some cases, traffickers were said to approach key individuals within transport service companies to corrupt. At other times, respondents noted a preference for 'planting' associated individuals in these organisations, to make savings on corruption costs. In still other cases, syndicates were said to establish transport, warehousing and logistics companies of their own, to assist in their operations.

In facilitating the passage of a shipment, corruption in such companies intersects with that among front-line law enforcement officials. Here, as noted by one respondent, 'traffickers have direct contact with clearing agents, handling agents and revenue officers: the entire system is coordinated' (GA-15, 2017[132]). This is clear from a number of the modus operandi most commonly witnessed. Respondents described cases where public and private collusion had seen canine units removed prior to the passage of a consignment (GA-12, 2017[57]) (NG-03, 2017[62]). In a similar modality, port and airport scanner attendants were reported to ensure machines are disabled or not manned at the crucial moment.

Other dispatch and inspection procedures were cited as presenting key corruption risks. Among other mechanisms, respondents described sealed containers tampered with, with contraband inserted prior to a consignment's dispatch. In other cases, contraband is said to have been inserted without touching the seal, prior to a customs officer signing the container off (GA-11, 2017[104]) (NG-07, 2017[112]) (NG-08, 2017[107]).

Falsification or obfuscation of shipment documentation was cited as a further risk. This can be done, respondents noted, by omitting to adequately or accurately disclose consignor, consignee or ownership information. In particular, inaccurate descriptions were highlighted as appearing on invoices and bills of lading were described as being switched, in order to hide the origin of the container and the identity of the sender and recipient. A further vulnerability was cited where containers are declared as empty; in such cases, they can be easier to move without completing formal checks – a factor cited as a vulnerability exploited by wildlife traffickers.

A further vulnerability was cited where officials are granted only partial access to key ports or airports. An example was cited in the case of Entebbe International Airport in Uganda: until a recent intervention from the President, UWA canine unit inspections could take place only in the main passenger section (Kaaya, 2017[133]). Numerous respondents, however, cited the VIP sections as particularly vulnerable to abuse (GA-11, 2017[104]) (GA-13, 2017[45]) (NG-18, 2017[38]). In a further indication of public–private collusion, a clearing firm handling logistics for a number of embassies in one focus country was claimed to have been pulled up for involvement (GA-11, 2017[104]) (GA-13, 2017[45]) (NG-18, 2017[38]).

4.3.4. Public and private connections and the risk of conflict of interest

Other respondents noted the importance of close personal relationships between public and private sectors. According to one, 'private sector corruption is often facilitated where individuals wear two hats – private and public. Family links in the two sectors are also highly relevant – corruption in the two sectors mixes and co-mingles' (NG-11, 2017[86]).

Lending support to this point are a number of recent alleged cases in Tanzania. These speak to both the potential intricacy of the links that can exist between the two sectors and the seniority of the officials that they can involve. One relevant case allegedly implicated a shipping company owned by a former secretary general of the ruling party in a 2009 shipment of 6.2 tonnes of ivory to Singapore (Box 4.2).

Box 4.2. High-Level Public and Private Sector Corruption Allegations in Tanzania

In 2014, EIA and the Economist published the results of investigations into the owner of a transport business and a series of hunting blocks near the Selous Game Reserve. The individual in question was also allegedly a donor to the ruling party, and a former member of the National Executive Committee (EIA, 2014[24]).

The individual concerned faced several accusations of dubious hunting practices. As noted by EIA in 2014, the individual in question owned (in full or in part) 16 hunting blocks in game reserves held by four different companies. As observed further by EIA, this would contravene national legislation on the maximum number of hunting concessions any one individual can lease.

In 2007, one of the individual's companies was allegedly implicated in illegally sub-letting a hunting block to other organisations. Despite this, the company allegedly retained its license and successfully obtained allocations for the period 2013–18 (EIA, 2014[24]) . In 2013 and 2014, reports indicated that the person in question exploited political and business connections to use hunting blocks for illegal poaching (Majani, 2013[134]) (Economist, 2014[135]).

4.3.5. Post-Arrest: The 'Chain of Corruption' in the Justice System

Across all transit-level corruption attempts described, the aim was cited as the same. All are designed to ensure that consignments pass chokepoints – undetected and unhindered. In some cases, however, interceptions are made, with corruption attempts misfiring. At this point, post-facto corruption is employed to ensure that those arrested get off. Here, corruption in the criminal justice system again comes into play, as described in Chapter 3.

Where it does, many of the structural vulnerabilities described previously are pro-actively exploited. An additional insight offered by respondents, however, concerns the 'chain' of corruption pursued as cases pass throughout the criminal justice system. This chain owes to the significant discrepancies in amounts of money required to corrupt at each level. To keep costs cheap, corruption attempts are held to be conducted from the bottom up – from arresting officers to investigating officers, to prosecutors and, ultimately, magistrates (GA-02, 2017[83]) (GA-04, 2017[37]) (GA-07, 2017[44]) (GA-14, 2017[106]). Such uni-directional targeting patterns are held to be dictated by the logic of 'cost saving'. Notably, respondents cited the significantly higher costs of interference at the highest level – the level of last resort. As one observed, 'The judiciary is at the helm – at the last stage of the chain. It takes a lot of money to bribe a judge' (GA-12, 2017[57]).

4.3.6. Species-Specific Supply-Chain Considerations

The above cases speak mainly to scenarios in which export and international transit activities are undertaken for wildlife products on Appendix I, such as ivory. However, corruption risks at transit level take diverse forms for species in which a parallel legal trade exists. Here, an awareness of such species' status under CITES is required to understand the varying corruption needs of those trafficking in these animals. CITES contains three separate appendices of species, and sets out the control mechanisms applicable to them. Appendix I includes species threatened with extinction in which commercial trade is not permitted. Appendix II includes species not necessarily in danger of extinction, but which may become endangered if trade is not strictly regulated. Species on Appendix II can thus be traded only under a permit system. Appendix III includes species protected by national legislation established by the country that added them to the CITES list.

Where species sit on Appendix I, corruption facilitates international trade in a product that is unambiguously illegal – like heroin or cocaine. Where species sit on Appendix II, meanwhile, greater ambiguities in legal status arise. For species in this category, corruption risks are held to emerge where this unclear status is exploited. The most common attempts to do so are held to revolve around the issuance, inspection and acceptance of CITES permits (NG-11, 2017[86]) (NG-13, 2017[73]) (NG-18, 2017[38]) (FD-06, 2017:[123]) . Such permits are required for species on CITES lists – to certify that the trade is not inconsistent with CITES protections.

4.3.7. Forgery of CITES permits

As noted in a 2017 OECD paper, 'The difference between a legal protected wildlife shipment and an illegal one boils down to paperwork' (OECD, 2017[136]). However, at present the permit system is not electronically run, with authorisations made using pen and paper. Although preparations for an electronic system are in the works, the current system remains highly vulnerable to abuse. At the same time, crucial vulnerabilities lie in the fact that paperwork remains non-standardised.

Respondents noted numerous cases where permits have been physically forged or falsified. In many, officials receive bribes to facilitate the process (NG-11, 2017[86]) (NG-13, 2017[73]) (NG-18, 2017[38]) (FD-06, 2017:[123]). Here, a key question revolves around the position of the officer responsible for issuing CITES paperwork. This can vary from country to country – with arrangements left to each party to CITES to agree. However, in many countries the official can be senior – at the level of the director of a wildlife management authority or minister for the environment, often on the recommendation of a wildlife management authority licensing officer (NG-03, 2017[62]) (NG-18, 2017[38]).

As such, greatest vulnerability was assessed to lie between mid-management and the highest levels of issuing institutions (NG-11, 2017[86]) (NG-13, 2017[73]) (NG-18, 2017[38]) (FD-06, 2017:[123]). Meanwhile, the likelihood of consequences for corrupt actions at this level are assessed to be limited. Indeed, corruption at this level is likely to be highly effective. As noted by the OECD, 'Once this export paperwork is in hand, with the exception of a limited number of well-resourced and conscientious countries, officials on the receiving end are unlikely to challenge it' (OECD, 2017[136]).

Indeed, given the high-level sign off often involved, respondents observed that contesting this paperwork would likely mean challenging the integrity of the issuing authority. As noted in 2017 by the OECD, for front-line customs inspectors in consumer states, 'the controversy sure to follow represents an ordeal few would be likely to voluntarily undertake'. At the same time, little motivation for them to raise objections exists, with any associated environmental harm having taken place in the permit-issuing country.

4.3.8. User Rights Licenses

Similarly mid-to-high-level responsibility often exists for issuance of permits for domestic use of key species. In Uganda, controversially, such permits have allegedly been issued in recent years to allow collection of pangolin scales and captive breeding of the animals themselves. These permits are sought in line with the Uganda Wildlife Act 1996, (Clause 30), which states that 'no person may engage in any of the activities under Section 29 (hunting, farming, ranching, trading in wildlife and wildlife products, and general extraction) … which involve the utilisation of wildlife and wildlife products without first obtaining a grant of a wildlife use right'. However, some respondents spoke of alleged irregular conditions in which such permits have recently been handed out (Box 4.3).

Box 4.3. Issuance of fraudulent permits for Pangolin Sales in Uganda

The case of a permit granted to a local company in July 2014 in Uganda has attracted attention. The permit allegedly permitted the company to collect 7,310 kg of Giant Pangolins from across the country (New Vision, 2015.[137]). The license was granted – as per request – not to collect live animals, but natural-mortality specimens accumulated by communities over the decades. However, authors Cakaj and Lezhnev note the apparent lack of supervision of the scales' collection (Cakaj and Lezhnev, 2017[29]). At the same time, the authors allege that the license ignored the fact that, according to Ugandan law, citizens are not permitted to possess wildlife.

As a result, the agreement was widely denounced as one that would trigger nationwide illegal pangolin killing. In 2015, a Uganda based NGO filed a civil suit against the wildlife management authority for its role in the affair. It did so alleging that, through its actions, a license to poach pangolins had effectively been issued (Kigongo, 2015[138]). In June 2015, however, Cakaj and Lezhnev report that the lawsuit was dismissed and the company was granted permission to export 1 metric ton of scales, for which it had obtained an export permit.

Meanwhile, Cakaj and Lezhnev have alleged that there were a number of other problems with this case. Specifically, they allege that the organisation was granted the permit in the absence of the issuance of a legal tender. Following its granting, they also allege that 150 kg of scales from UWA stores were handed over to the company in spite of the status of some as exhibits in an ongoing case against poachers (Cakaj and Lezhnev, 2017[29]).

Beyond the example in Box 4.3, respondents highlighted other cases in which the granting of formal user rights licenses has the potential to mask illegitimate activity. Here, they cited a proposal from the Asia-Africa Pangolin Breeding Research Centre Limited to conduct 'experimental research on captive breeding of pangolins in Uganda' (IUCN-SSC, 2016[139]). The potential risks involved in this proposal attracted international attention. In September 2016, the IUCN Species Survival Commission Pangolin Specialist Group and African Pangolin Working Group wrote a letter expressing concern over the proposed breeding programme.

Specifically, these bodies laid out their fears that the programme could be used to launder illegally killed animals into legal supply chains. Here, they observe that high mortality rates, slow reproductive rates and the costs involved in housing and feeding the animals make it 'difficult to see the investment value in such a proposition'. In light of this, they note that 'farming wildlife actually increases the hunting pressure to supply wild animals to the farms'. 'It is impossible to accurately distinguish wild pangolins from farmed pangolins', they go on to note; 'ultimately, the risk associated with taking wild pangolins into captivity is too high' (IUCN-SSC, 2016[139]) . Heeding this advice, the proposal was ultimately rejected.

4.3.9. Hunting Licences

Such issues around captive breeding appear to be of greater concern in Uganda than in other focus countries. Elsewhere, however, similar license-based issues arise around the issuance of permits for professional hunting. Both Tanzania and Zambia maintain large-scale and active legal hunting industries. Concerns were expressed by respondents in both countries over the IWT-linked corruption risks embodied within them.

In Tanzania, for example, concerns have been expressed over the influence of corruption on the country's tourist hunting industry since the early 1970s. A key vulnerability was highlighted by respondents around the process of allocation of hunting blocks and licenses. In a 2009 article, Leader-Williams et al. expressed concern around the integrity of 'decisions of mid- to senior-level staff in the Wildlife Department's headquarters that set quotas, issue licences, collect fees and allocate most hunting blocks' (Leader-Williams et al, 2009[22]). A similar concern was expressed by respondents in Zambia, where respondents spoke of the strong competition for the allocation of concessions.

Here, respondents noted that 'corruption is used to ensure that those in charge of allocations favour certain sectors or individuals. There are only a limited number of concessions available; bribes are paid to secure them' (GA-17-2017, 2017[63]). In Zambia concessions typically last 10 years, at which point retendering processes take place. Numerous respondents cited the regular scandals emerging around these processes, resulting in corruption allegations and dismissals (Box 4.4).

Box 4.4. Corruption allegations around former Tourism and Arts Minister in Zambia

In July 2015, Zambia's Anti-Corruption Commission arrested a former Minister of Tourism and Arts, charging them with two counts of alleged abuse of authority of office during their time as minister (Lusaka Times, 2017[140]). On the first count, the Minister was accused of allegedly cancelling the procurement of a tender process of ZAWA hunting concessions without following due procedure. On the second count, the Minister was accused of alleged abuse of office for terminating the employment of senior ZAWA officers, again without adhering to due process.

The Minister pleaded 'not guilty' and in July 2017 was acquitted by the Lusaka Magistrates Court. The Minister charged in her final submission to the court that they had been engaged in fighting entrenched corruption within ZAWA, and alleged that the tender process that was cancelled had seen numerous irregularities. The Minister accused the Anti-Corruption Commission of failing to act on the reports submitted around these issues (Phiri, 2017[141]).

These processes can be affected by political interference. As noted by Leader-Williams et al. in Tanzania, 'of equal concern is patronage and nepotism involving senior politicians' (Leader-Williams et al, 2009[22]). The authors note that 'perhaps the least tractable [issue] is the most senior politicians offering exclusive rights to foreigners presumably considered to be of financial or other strategic importance.' Box 4.5 provides a telling example highlighted by respondents of the latter scenario.

Box 4.5. Granting of Tanzania hunting concessions to UAE Royal family and subsequent investigation by PCCB

Respondents cited the controversial granting in Tanzania of hunting rights in the 1990s to a company owned by the UAE royal family. In November 2017, the 25-year-old concession was revoked amid investigations into interactions between the company and former Tanzanian Tourism Ministers. These saw the Natural Resources Minister order the PCCB to investigate the owner of the company in question and suspend the director of wildlife. News outlets alleged that financial donations had been received from the royal family in previous years: a report noted that the ruling party had received $32,000 in donations in 1994 and the Ministry of Natural Resources and Tourism more than $2 million. Fears were expressed around the number of animals killed in the interim years, including of potentially endangered species. However, these allegations are not substantiated (Kabendera, 2017[142]).

The example provided in Box 4.5 points to less overt forms of corruption that may take place among higher levels in government. These can occur when there is inadequate supervision of quotas issued to regulate the hunting of particular species on assigned blocks. As noted by one respondent, 'The management of concessions is a significant 'blind spot': the government is not effectively monitoring hunting to quotas' (GA-18, 2017[52]). In theory, scouts are required to monitor hunting activity on concessions, with responsibility for measuring and recording animal and trophy size for each kill. In practice, they are alleged to be paid-off to look the other way. Here, some respondents spoke of the potentially greater vulnerability embodied in smaller-scale relative to larger-scale professional hunting operations, where fewer resources in the way of monitors may be assigned.

Other respondents spoke of the risk of under-declaration of particular species relative to actual numbers hunted – to ensure that records align with quotas. As observed by one, 'quotas are not well monitored and hunting/export permit provisions often exceed stated quotas' (GA-18, 2017[52]). In other cases, respondents reported the issuance by wealthy clients of illegal payments for quotas to be increased. Others still reported measures to 'get around' quota issues – including baiting particular animals onto or off game ranches or national parks. Here, the position of many key locations on national borders was held to create further vulnerabilities, potentially providing an additional transit route for illegally hunted wildlife.

4.3.10. Illegal Trade in Live Animals

In cases in which quotas are exceeded, the main concern expressed by respondents related to the illegal killing of protected wildlife, which can then be exported in dead parts. However, related concerns have been raised over trade in live animals captured in violation of regulations. This may occur domestically: respondents raised questions around cases in which officials had allegedly illegally wild-captured animals inside national parks, to supply game ranges and luxury lodges (GA-18, 2017[52]). At other times, such illegal wild-capture incidents have allegedly been undertaken to supply international buyers. In such cases, the illegal international trade this enables can take on more significant implications under CITES.

Several live export issues were reported in Tanzania. In November 2010, for example, over 100 animals were reportedly illegally exported on a military plane from Kilimanjaro International Airport to Qatar (Mjema, 2013[143]). The animals reportedly included giraffes, lions, gazelles, hornbills, vultures, among other species. A witness to the case reported that the loading process was overseen by a Pakistani national and the pilot of the plane. He also reported that three giraffes, along with other animals, had died in their cages following capture, and that further animals were stolen to compensate for the loss.

Following the incident, the Pakistani national was put on Interpol's Most Wanted list of suspects of environmental crimes (Guardian, 2014[144]). Meanwhile, a number of high-level Tanzanian officials were accused of involvement. In 2012, two individuals from the Tanzania CITES management Authority were accused, and later in 2014, the then-director of wildlife. All were dismissed for their alleged involvement in the acts (Cota-Larson, 2012[145]) (Reuters, 2014[146]).

Such issues may affect Tanzania disproportionately, owing to the country's significant size and biodiversity. As noted by one respondent, 'High levels of endemism in Tanzania make the illegal pet trade a bigger issue than elsewhere'. The forms of corruption facilitating this are also distinctive, in a number of ways.

First, as in the live export cases described above, the distinctness of associated corruption lies in the different requirements to facilitate movement of live animals. Here, officers such as official vets are held up as more likely to be involved (NG-07, 2017[112]) (NG-11, 2017[86]) (NG-25, 2017[90]) (IE-05, 2017[55]). Second, as for some other forms of IWT, the presence of both a legal and illegal trade facilitates corruption. Indeed, a legal pet trade exists, with a number of companies involved legally in live pet exports. However, knowledge and awareness of the difference between common and highly endangered animals and birds may be highly limited on the part of officials. Where sufficient knowledge exists, meanwhile, corruption may be employed to forge paperwork – which, again, is mostly paper-based (NG-11, 2017[86]) (NG-13, 2017[73]) (NG-18, 2017[38]) (FD-06, 2017:[123]).

4.3.11. Diversity of Corruption throughout the Trade Chain

The corruption risks highlighted so far demonstrate the diversity and complexity of the situation across the focus countries. Whether at poaching level, transportation level or in the criminal justice system, corruption risks assume a range of forms.

In presenting this variety of risks, a majority of respondents highlighted the differences in the nature of the likely experiences of those affected. At the top end, the amounts of money involved are substantial, with officials not dependent on them for their economic wellbeing. At the bottom end of the chain, by contrast, respondents noted the very different drivers involved where officers engage in corrupt actions. Here, they describe the very survival issues often involved in decisions to engage. As noted by one respondent, 'ground level officers' salaries are too low: if they want to survive, they have no option but to bring in additional income from other sources. If they received a reasonable income this would change: in many cases, the individuals affected would rather be rangers than poachers.' (NG-12, 2017[91])

Another concluded: 'it is very difficult to look at corruption of the kind a ranger might engage in one minute, and the kind a minister might engage in the next. The drivers and incentives are entirely different and it's uncomfortable to put both in the same hat' (NG-11, 2017[86]). This analysis supports the diversity and complexity of experiences reported in interviews for this report. It also raises the question of responses – and particularly the most effective ways to engage with all levels of actor and institution facing corruption risk. Chapter 5 presents the perspectives of interviewees on this issue – detailing proposals made for the most effective responses across the focus countries.

References

Cakaj, L. and S. Lezhnev (2017), *Deadly Profits: Illegal Wildlife Trafficking through Uganda and South Sudan*.

CITES (2017), "Status of Elephant Populations, Levels of Illegal Killing and the Trade in Ivory: A Report to the CITES Standing Committee", Vol. SC69 Doc. 51.1 Annex, p. p. 3, https://cites.org/sites/default/files/eng/com/sc/69/E-SC69-51-01-A.pdf.

Cota-Larson, R. (2012), "Tanzania: Wildlife Officials Fired for Animal Trafficking", https://annamiticus.com/2012/08/15/tanzania-wildlife-officials-fired-for-animal-trafficking/.

Deutsche Welle (2017), *Rangers colluding with elephant poachers in Tanzania*, http://www.dw.com/en/rangers-colluding-with-elephant-poachers-in-tanzania/av-41837902.

Economist (2014), *Big Game Poachers*.

EIA (2017), *The Shuidong Connection: Exposing the Global Hub of the Illegal Ivory Trade*, https://eia-international.org/wp-content/uploads/EIA-The-Shuidong-Connection-FINAL.pdf.

EIA (2015), *Targeting wildlife crime bosses – it's all about the money*, https://eia-international.org/targeting-wildlife-crime-bosses-its-all-about-the-money.

FD-04 (2017), "REPRESENTATIVE OF FOREIGN DELEGATION 7: Environmental Affairs Advisor at Foreign Delegation, in person interview, Wednesday 6 September 2017".

FD-06 (2017:), "REPRESENTATIVE OF FOREIGN DELEGATION 10: Environmental Affairs advisor, in person interview, Monday 11 December 2017".

Findley et al. (2012), *Global Shell Games: Testing Money Launderers' and Terrorist Financiers' Access to Shell Companies*, http://www.michael-findley.com/uploads/2/0/4/5/20455799/oct2012-global-shell-games.media-summary.10oct12.pdf..

GA-01 (2017), "REPRESENTATIVES OF GOVERNMENT AGENCY 1, 2, 3, 4: In person interview, Thursday 7 September".

GA-01 (2017), "REPRESENTATIVES OF GOVERNMENT AGENCY 1, 2, 3, 4: In person interview, Thursday 7 September,".

GA-02 (2017), "REPRESENTATIVE OF GOVERNMENT AGENCY 5: In Person interview Thursday 7 September, BY PHONE".

GA-03 (2017), "REPRESENTATIVE OF GOVERNMENT AGENCY 6: In person interview, Friday 8 September, 2017".

GA-04 (2017), "REPRESENTATIVE OF GOVERNMENT AGENCY 7: In person Interview, Friday 8 September, 2017".

GA-05 (2017), "REPRESENTATIVE OF GOVERNMENT AGENCY 8: In person interview, Wednesday 13 December 2017".

GA-06 (2017), "REPRESENTATIVE OF GOVERNMENT AGENCY 9: In person interview, Thursday 14 December 2017".

GA-07 (2017), "REPRESENTATIVES OF GOVERNMENT AGENCY 10, 11: In person interview, Friday 15 December 2017".

GA-09 (2017), "REPRESENTATIVES OF GOVERNMENT AGENCY 14, 15: In person Interview, Friday 15 December 2017".

GA-10 (2017), "REPRESENTATIVE OF GOVERNMENT AGENCY 16: In person interview, Sunday 3 September 2017".

GA-11 (2017), "REPRESENTATIVES OF GOVERNMENT AGENCY 17, 18, 19: In person interview, Tuesday 5 September 2017".

GA-12 (2017), "REPRESENTATIVES OF GOVERNMENT AGENCY 20, 21: In person interview, Tuesday 5 September 2017".

GA-13 (2017), "REPRESENTATIVE OF GOVERNMENT AGENCY 22: In person interview, Tuesday 5 September,".

GA-14 (2017), "REPRESENTATIVE OF GOVERNMENT AGENCY 23: In person interview, Wednesday 6 September 2017".

GA-15 (2017), "REPRESENTATIVE OF GOVERNMENT AGENCY 24: In person interview, Wednesday 6 September 2017".

GA-17-2017 (2017), "REPRESENTATIVE OF GOVERNMENT AGENCY 25: In person interview, Monday 11 December 2017".

GA-18 (2017), "REPRESENTATIVES OF GOVERNMENT AGENCY 27, 27, 28, 29: In person interview, Tuesday 12 December 2017".

GA-20 (2017), "REPRESENTATIVES OF GOVERNMENT AGENCY 31, 32: In person Interview, Tuesday 12 December 2017".

Great Elephant Census (2016), "Zambia Census Results Announced: Luangwa and Kafue Stable, Lower Zambezi Declines and Sioma Ngwezi Declines Catastrophically", http://www.greatelephantcensus.com/blog/2016/3/2/zambia-census-announced-luangwa-and-kafue-stable-lower-zambezi-and-sioma-ngwezi-see-decline.

Guardian (2014), "Interpol Launches First Appeal for Environmental Fugitives", https://www.theguardian.com/environment/2014/nov/17/interpol-launches-first-appeal-for-environmental-fugitives.

IE-02-2017 (2017), "INDEPENDENT EXPERT 2: In person interview, Saturday 9 September 2017".

IE-03 (2017), "INDEPENDENT EXPERT 3: In person interview, Monday 11 September, 2017".

IE-05 (2017), "INDEPENDENT EXPERT 5: In person interview, Monday 11 December 2017".

IUCN-SSC (2016), "Uganda: Refuse plans to farm pangolins, say wildlife expert", *IUCN-SSC Pangolin Specialist Group*, http://animalpeopleforum.org/2016/09/27/uganda-refuse-plans-to-farm-pangolins-say-wildlife-experts/..

Kaaya, S. (2017), *Museveni orders use of sniffer dogs to track VIPs*, http://observer.ug/news/headlines/54627-museveni-orders-use-of-sniffer-dogs-to-track-vips.html.

Kabendera, E. (2017), "Tanzania ends hunting deal with Dubai royal family'", *The East African*, http://www.theeastafrican.co.ke/news/Tanzania-ends-hunting-deal-with-Dubai-royal-family/2558-4182470-dv6hysz/index.html.

Kigongo, J. (2015), *UWA sued over export of pangolin scales*, http://www.monitor.co.ug/News/National/UWA-sued-over-export-of-pangolin-scales/688334-2605462-xtbr6kz/index.html..

Koech, G. (2017), *'Elephant poaching declines in Kenya, focus turns to world markets'*, https://www.the-star.co.ke/news/2017/11/30/elephant-poaching-declines-in-kenya-focus-turns-to-world-markets_c1677846.

Leader-Williams et al (2009), "The Influence of Corruption on the Conduct of Recreational Hunting", *Conservation and Rural Livelihoods: Science and Practice*.

Lusaka Times (2017), "Court Acquits Former Tourism Minister Sylvia Masebo on Charges of Abuse of Authority", https://www.lusakatimes.com/2017/07/14/court-acquits-former-tourism-minister-sylvia-masebo-charges-abuse-authority/.

Majani, F. (2013), *Corrupt officials ensure the battle against poaching remains futile'*, https://mg.co.za/article/2013-08-08-00-corrupt-officials-ensure-the-battle-against-poaching-remains-futile.

Mathiesen, K. (2015), "Tanzania elephant population declined by 60% in five years, census reveals", *Guardian*, http://dx.doi.org/Tanzania elephant population declined by 60% in five years, census reveals'.

Miller et al. (2015), *Species of Crime: Typologies and Risk Metrics for Wildlife Trafficking*, https://static1.squarespace.com/static/566ef8b4d8af107232d5358a/t/56af8242cf80a1474b572b85/1454342724100/Species+of+Crime.pdf.

Mjema, D. (2013), "Witness recalls how giraffes, elands were sneaked out of KIA", *The Citizen*, http://www.thecitizen.co.tz/News/national/How-we-stole-your-giraffes/1840392-2094446-q3n8rbz/index.html..

MNRT (2017), "CITES National Ivory Action Plan Progress Report. Reporting period: 1st January 2017 – 31st December 2017'", *Tanzania Ministry of Natural Resources and Tourism.*

Namaiko, C. (2014), *Thieves Raid ZAWA... K1m Worth of Ivory Tusks Stolen*, http://www.times.co.zm/?p=46733.

New Vision (2015.), *UWA clears export of sh11b pangolin scales.*

NG-01 (2017), "REPRESENTATIVE OF WILDLIFE NGO 1: In person Interview, Thursday 7 September,".

NG-03 (2017), "REPRESENTATIVE OF NGO 3: in person interview, Friday 8 September, 2017".

NG-07 (2017), "REPRESENTATIVE OF NGO 7: In person interview, Monday 11 September 2017".

NG-08 (2017), "REPRESENTATIVE OF NGO 33: In person interview, Monday 11 September, 2017".

NG-09 (2017), "REPRESENTATIVE OF NGO 34: in person interview, Monday 11 September 2017".

NG-10 (2017), "REPRESENTATIVES OF NGO 8, 9: In person interview, Wednesday 13 December 2017".

NG-11 (2017), "REPRESENTATIVE OF NGO 10: In person interview, Thursday 14 December 2017".

NG-12 (2017), "REPRESENTATIVE OF NGO 11: In person interview, 14 December 2017".

NG-13 (2017), "REPRESENTATIVE OF NGO 12: In person interview, 14 December 2017".

NG-14 (2017), "REPRESENTATIVES OF NGO 13, 14: In person interview, Thursday 14 December 2017".

NG-17 (2017), "REPRESENTATIVE OF NGO 19, 20: In person interview, Monday 4 September, 2017".

NG-18 (2017), "REPRESENTATIVE OF NGO 21: In person interview, Tuesday 5 September,".

NG-19 (2017), "REPRESENTATIVE OF NGO 22: In person interview, Wednesday 6 September 2017".

NG-20 (2017), "REPRESENTATIVE OF NGO 23: In person interview, Wednesday 6 September 2017".

NG-21 (2017), "REPRESENTATIVES OF NGO 24, 25: In person interview, Monday 11 December 2017".

NG-23 (2017), "REPRESENTATIVES OF NGO 27, 28: In person interview, Tuesday 12 December 2017".

NG-24 (2017), "REPRESENTATIVE OF NGO 29, 30: Skype interview, 15 December 2017".

NG-25 (2017), "REPRESENTATIVE OF NGO 31: Skype interview, Wednesday 20 December, 2017".

OECD (2017), *Corruption and Wildlife Crime: 5th OECD Taskforce on Countering Illicit Trade.*

Phiri, C. (2017), "Masebo Acquitted of Corruption'", *Zambia Reports*, https://zambiareports.com/2017/07/14/masebo-acquitted-corruption/.

PS-01 (2017), "REPRESENTATIVE OF PRIVATE SECTOR INSTITUTION 1: In person Interview,

Tuesday 5 September,".

Reuters (2014), "Tanzania sacks top wildlife officials over animal smuggling", https://www.reuters.com/article/us-tanzania-wildlife/tanzania-sacks-top-wildlife-officials-over-animal-smuggling-idUSBRE87D0QS20120814;.

Smith, D. (2016), *Kenya burns largest ever ivory stockpile to highlight elephants' fate*, https://www.theguardian.com/environment/2016/apr/30/kenya-to-burn-largest-ever-ivory-stockpile-to-highlight-elephants-fate.

Vaughan, A. (2016), *Kenya's new front in poaching battle: "the future is in the hands of our communities"*, https://www.theguardian.com/environment/2016/may/30/kenya-poaching-elephant-ivory-rhino-horn-future-communities.

Wasser et al. (2015), "Genetic Assignment of Large Seizures of Elephant Ivory Reveals Africa's Major Poaching Hotspots", *Science*.

Wolpert, S. (2015), *Which is most valuable: Gold, cocaine or rhino horn?*, http://newsroom.ucla.edu/releases/which-is-most-valuable-gold-cocaine-or-rhino-horn.

Zambia Reports (2012), *Massive Theft of Ivory Causes Scandal in Zambia*, https://zambiareports.com/2012/06/20/massive-theft-of-ivory-causes-scandal-in-zambia/.

Zambian Watchdog (2012), *Police detain journalists, torture suspects in Ivory stolen by PF bosses*, http://dx.doi.org/www.zambiawatchdog.com/police-detain-journalists-torture-suspects-in-ivory-stolen-by-pf-bosses/.

Note

[1] The situation is complicated in countries like Uganda, where – under the Special Wildlife Integrated Force for Tourism (SWIFT) – military officers are seconded to UWA and are employed as UWA rangers.

5. IWT and Corruption Risks: Responses

This chapter provides a summary of the existing interventions against IWT employed by the various public authorities working on anti-corruption in the focus countries. The report highlights the existing strengths and best practices identified in the four countries. It also notes the common gaps that require further attention to mitigate corruption risks.

'Whilst corruption is capable of affecting many aspects of conservation, this does not imply that its effects are universal and endemic.' (Smith and Walpole, 2005[18])

In light of the corruption risks highlighted in Chapters 3 and 4, an important question arises around how domestic and international stakeholders can engage in programming that is attuned to these risks. Interviewees provided a range of views on the need for specific interventions in this regard; these responses form the basis of this chapter. First, respondents highlighted the gaps in existing IWT programming when it comes to mitigating corruption risks. Secondly, they made proposals for targeted interventions designed to tackle corruption linked to IWT head on.

5.1. Gaps in Existing IWT Interventions

From the outset, respondents emphasised the need to tailor IWT programming to the specific corruption risks witnessed in each focus country. In doing so, they pointed to the need to undertake structured corruption risk assessments specifically tailored to each country's fight against IWT. These assessments should be a prerequisite to intervention – they must not be treated as add-ons. Specifically, respondents insisted that risk-assessment and -management measures be positioned as a central component of broader counter-wildlife trafficking and conservation interventions (Williams et al., 2016[17]).

To date, donors and NGOs have not adopted significant anti-corruption agendas in their work. Where they have engaged with relevant public-sector agencies, support often takes the form of material support, capacity building and training.[1] The effects of such initiatives can be positive: further professionalization, training and better equipment can result in greater institutional capacities. Nevertheless, in some cases, respondents spoke of the existence of inadequate assurances that financing or material support did not in fact increase the risks of corruption. This has reportedly been the case in a number of donor-funded support programmes: in such cases, donor spending is said to inadvertently have facilitated corruption in key locations. (NG-11, 2017[86]) (NG-12, 2017[91]) (NG-13, 2017[73])

The need to ensure that interventions do not fuel corruption was emphasised by respondents – particularly from international organisations and NGOs – in the strongest terms (NG-11, 2017[86]) (NG-12, 2017[91]) (NG-13, 2017[73]) (IE-03, 2017[124]) (IO-01, 2017[61]). Beyond this, many spoke of the need for new interventions not only to 'do no harm' in relation to fuelling corruption – but to take proactive steps to address corruption through specific, focused programming (GA-02, 2017[83]) (NG-12, 2017[91]) (NG-13, 2017[73]) (NG-18, 2017[38]) (IE-01, 2017[147]) (IO-01, 2017[61]). According to one respondent, we need a 'wholesale shift' in the way we respond to IWT, in which 'corruption is placed front and centre'. (NG-03, 2017[62]). Another respondent noted that 'if donors and other actors in this space do not invest in anti-corruption activities in parallel to counter-IWT work, they may as well go home' (NG-18, 2017[38]).

A number of NGOs have strengthened their focus on anti-corruption efforts in an attempt to fill this gap. One – the EAGLE Network (see Box 5.1) – has adopted an explicit anti-corruption focus, noting that in 85% of field operations involving interdictions and arrests and in 80% of all court cases, bribes are offered in exchange for release or exemptions. For this reason, the network champions a proactive approach to addressing corruption in any efforts to counter IWT. It describes itself further not simply as an observer of corruption, but a network 'created to fight corruption, redirecting the positive pressures ... within the system ... to specific corruption attempts' (EAGLE Network, 2018[148]).

However, on the whole, NGOs engaged in explicitly anti-corruption work are small in number.

Box 5.1. EAGLE Network Anticorruption Programming leads to convictions of officials in Uganda

The NGO EAGLE Network laments the fact that most donor funding 'is focused on "capacity building" without any diagnosis [of] whether "lack of capacity" is indeed the problem'. EAGLE notes that 'increasing [the] capacity of a corrupt system is not only ineffective but counter-productive'. The problem, it argues, lies in a lack of appropriate standards to measure impact, allowing the '"capacity building approach" to continue regardless of its lack of results'. Instead, EAGLE points to 'governance' as a larger problem than lack of capacity, urging donors to switch from a 'capacity building' to a 'governance building' approach. 'Governance building' measures, it notes, can range from developing whistle-blower programmes, to developing stronger internal reporting structures within relevant agencies, to introducing systems that track outcomes and accountabilities (EAGLE Network, 2018[148]).

In pursuing such a 'governance building' approach, EAGLE seeks to 'follow up the entire law enforcement process from investigation to jail visits to confirm execution of sentences' in a 'body-guard system against corruption'.

Among numerous other successes, in January 2017, EAGLE activity led to the arrest of a senior presidential adviser with 183 kg of hippo teeth in his vehicle. In March 2017, EAGLE also announced the arrests for wildlife trafficking of three officials from the UPDF, Uganda Police Force and Uganda Prison Services. (EAGLE Network, 2018[148])

5.2. Proposals for Targeted Anti-Corruption Interventions

In addition to such direct, operations-focused interventions as those undertaken by EAGLE, respondents cited a range of other potential measures to build governance. In doing so, many cited the need to adopt a preventative approach – mitigating corruption risks before they arise (IO-01, 2017[61]) (IO-02, 2017[42]) (NG-20, 2017[39]) (RI-01, 2017[76]). Prevention is particularly important in the wildlife sector (where resources are finite and irreplaceable once exhausted). In pursuing such a preventative approach, respondents highlighted a number of opportunities for intervention. These exist in the sourcing stage, through the transit stage, and across the criminal justice system. A number of these opportunities are listed below.

5.2.1. Automation and technological innovations

At sourcing stage, respondents stressed the need to target corruption risks within front-line agencies charged with protecting wildlife. Here, many cited the importance of automation as a means to remove discretion – and opportunity – from vulnerable field-level officers (GA-13, 2017[45]) (IE-03, 2017[124]) (NG-14, 2017[108]). From the perspective of graft and corruption, automation of park-entry fees can be effective innovations: for example, KWS introduced electronic ticketing in January 2017. This has transformed park entry into a cashless system, with options for payment via mobile money and bank transfer. As noted by a respondent close to the process, 'this has ensured that there is no direct contract between gatekeepers and entry fees. It has had a positive impact on revenue collection and has reduced embezzlement, ensuring both administrative efficiency and anti-corruption outcomes' (GA-03, 2017[99]).

Automation presents numerous other opportunities as a corruption reduction strategy, including through the potential use of electronic licensing processes. For example, respondents highlighted the need to develop a global electronic CITES permitting system. Such a system would reduce corruption risks around the physical forgery, and unauthorised use, of non-standardised paper-based permits. Importantly, it would also enable the establishment of a centralised database of CITES records, which could be used to investigate irregularities and address accountability gaps. Furthermore, the system would assist in tracing and investigating import and export discrepancies that may arise (NG-11, 2017[86]) (NG-13, 2017[73]) (NG-18, 2017[38]) (IO-02, 2017[42]) (FD-06, 2017:[123]).

Keeping closer track of the whereabouts of officers is another important part of increasing accountability, particularly in a context where parks cover large expanses. Respondents cited the need to use dedicated equipment to track in real time ranger patrols – thus reducing discretion in undertaking and reporting patrol patterns. Technological solutions are also needed to protect and secure radio communications, to prevent criminal networks from becoming aware of the location of patrols – and to prevent corrupt rangers from providing radio equipment or other forms of technological assistance to poachers (NG-24, 2017[89]).

5.2.2. Changing Incentive Structures at Source Level

Field officers can be drawn to, or driven from corruption depending on the incentive structures in place (GA-06, 2017[103]) (NG-06, 2017[58]) (NG-12, 2017[91]) (NG-23, 2017[53]). As noted by one respondent, 'It is crucial, wherever possible, to incentivise officers not to go to the wrong side' (NG-12, 2017[91]). Some respondents agreed on the need to increase pay scales for relatively underpaid officers. Others pointed to irregular pay schemes for some officers, particularly locally engaged staff in remote locations. In addition, respondents spoke of the need for interventions to address morale more broadly, whether by improving equipment, accommodation or rangers' ability to play their part in the criminal justice chain (GA-01, 2017[82]) (GA-06, 2017[103]) (NG-24, 2017[89]).

In particular, respondents raised the need to address such risks where government delegates authority to scouts. In a scenario, often, of low support and low morale, field scouts are viewed as particularly vulnerable to corruption. However, where relatively stable pay, stronger morale and better-established incentive structures can be ensured, scouts have been shown to perform their duties more effectively. Where capacities to provide such conditions are limited, respondents noted that NGOs can play a role in filling the gap. Citing their own field experience, certain NGOs spoke of positive experience in this regard. One NGO related particular success in the provision of technical and ethics-based training to local scout teams that support rangers, providing financial incentive structures alongside this to reward reporting. Another NGO described the institution of a successful local reward system, with scouts and community members rewarded for information leading to arrests of wildlife criminals (NG-14, 2017[108]).

5.3. Addressing Corruption Risks: Internal Integrity Mechanisms and Links to Anti-Corruption Authorities

Focusing more centrally, certain respondents from government, international organisations and NGOs stressed the need to bolster anti-corruption and integrity mechanisms within wildlife management authorities (GA-08, 2017[36]) (IO-01, 2017[61]) (IO-02, 2017[42]) (NG-12, 2017[91]). As noted by one respondent, 'it is vital that more pressure is placed on the internal policing of wildlife agencies'. (NG-06, 2017[58]). On a related point, respondents spoke of the need to review hiring practices, conduct advanced background checks and establish vetted units in particular areas (GA-03, 2017[99]) (GA-08, 2017[36]) (NG-12, 2017[91]) (NG-18, 2017[38]). They also stressed the need to reform and re-invigorate broader internal integrity mechanisms (GA-08, 2017[36]) (IO-01, 2017[61]) (IO-02, 2017[42]) (NG-12, 2017[91]). It was stressed that this must be done on a broad scale, addressing all corruption risks within a particular wildlife management authority writ large. As observed by one respondent, 'it is impossible to look at corruption linked to IWT without looking at the broader culture of an organisation' (NG-03, 2017[62]).

In recognition of this risk, UNODC is currently engaged in the provision of policy support to anti-corruption measures within KWS. Much of this work has focused on strengthening the Service's Corruption Prevention Committee – a multi-departmental body drawing staff from a range of branches. The committee has placed importance on ensuring field-level involvement, with the views of senior wardens across Kenya sought and incorporated. At the same time, KWS plans to develop local Corruption Prevention Committees, to monitor the situation in local areas. Such decentralisation ensures that whistle-blower and other integrity mechanisms 'have tentacles close to the ground' (IO-01, 2017[61]).

Meanwhile, with UNODC support, KWS is prioritizing a review of key corruption risks across the Service, in functions from procurement to HR to asset management. KWS is also amending and reviewing key documents, such as the KWS Standing Orders and Disciplinary Code. (KWS, 2017[149]). The review of the latter will seek to address key vulnerabilities, while aligning the document with the Wildlife Conservation and Management Act, 2013. In July 2017, the acting Director General expressed his 'optimism that the initiative will produce a comprehensive document that addresses all facets of discipline among…uniformed staff' (KWS, 2017[149]). Similar policy work is underway in Tanzania, with UNODC supporting the NCAA, TAWA and TANAPA.

Many respondents cited this strengthening of internal policy as fundamental to corruption prevention (GA-08, 2017[36]) (IO-01, 2017[61]) (IO-02, 2017[42]) (NG-12, 2017[91]) (NG-13, 2017[73]). However, in Uganda and Zambia, similar work has not been undertaken on the same scale, with respondents noting the need for additional support (IO-02, 2017[42]) (NG-03, 2017[62]). Meanwhile, even where policy work has taken place, respondents observed that success would ultimately lie in implementation – both in the field and at HQ level (IO-02, 2017[42]) (NG-03, 2017[62]). As noted by one respondent, engagement from the highest levels is necessary to the success of anti-corruption codes and policies: 'This is all about organisational culture. You won't have the right culture if the leadership is not supportive and does not understand the value of the work' (NG-03, 2017[62]).

This point speaks again to the importance of hierarchy in changing organisational culture. As noted by one respondent, 'the response [to corruption] needs to be largely top-down; it is not useful to go after the bottom levels if the higher levels are on the take' (NG-11,

2017[86]). As observed by one respondent 'a "conducive environment" for anti-corruption strategies is crucial – and can only be set at high levels' (GA-06, 2017[103]). Part of this high-level will, others noted, must lie in a willingness to admit and deal seriously with internal corruption problems when they arise. This must involve fostering closer operational ties with anti-corruption authorities.

As such, beyond internal policy shifts, respondents cited the need to address institutional disconnects with anti-corruption bodies (GA-04, 2017[37]) (GA-08, 2017[36]) (GA-19, 2017[56]) (NG-06, 2017[58]) (NG-07, 2017[112]) (NG-21, 2017[59]). These respondents stressed the need to ensure that cases are referred to anti-corruption authorities on a systematic basis when criminal acts are suspected, instead of relying on internal disciplinary actions. However, anti-corruption authorities typically do not have extensive amount of expertise in the field of corruption related to the wildlife sector (GA-18, 2017[52]) (NG-20, 2017[39]) (IE-05, 2017[55]). As a result, several respondents noted that further training is necessary to enhance anti-corruption officers' knowledge and awareness on wildlife issues (NG-04, 2017[97]) (NG-18, 2017[38]) (NG-20, 2017[39]).

5.4. Addressing Corruption Risks: Multi-Agency Structures and Public–Private Partnerships

Many respondents noted that multi-agency coordination could foster exchanges of expertise, sharing of knowledge and accountability structures that would assist in the fight against corruption. The exchange of information on cases, typologies and drawing connections between cases can assist all parties to ensure that the agencies affected are aware of the necessary steps to be taken in any particular case (GA-04, 2017[37]) (GA-08, 2017[36]) (GA-19, 2017[56]) (NG-06, 2017[58]) (NG-07, 2017[112]) (NG-21, 2017[59]).

Beyond this, direct cooperation between agencies in the form of inter-agency secondment and exchanges are valuable tools to exchange knowledge between anti-corruption and other agencies (GA-01, 2017[82]) (GA-07, 2017[44]) (GA-12, 2017[57]) (NG-18, 2017[38]) (NG-19, 2017[100]). For example, as noted by one respondent speaking from within an anti-corruption authority, 'a much-needed response would be to fund the anti-corruption authority to embed investigators within the wildlife management authority'. This would allow specialised anti-corruption actors 'to look specifically into official facilitation of IWT' (IE-01, 2017[147]).

At the same time, respondents noted the value of multi-agency structures in countering corruption linked to IWT. According to one participant, structures such as the NTAP (Box 5.2) 'create stronger checks and balances, by mixing agencies and thus enhancing accountability' (GA-07, 2017[44]). As a multi-agency structure, they noted that all members of such units have reporting structures that are de-centralised, and decisions cannot be carried out by a single administration without other agencies' knowledge or involvement (GA-07, 2017[44]) (NG-12, 2017[91]). As such, with different heads both within and outside the taskforce, 'individuals have significantly wider options for reporting potential corruption' (GA-07, 2017[44]).

Box 5.2. Multi-Agency Responses: Tanzania's National Taskforce Anti-Poaching

To address the vulnerabilities that arise from working in 'silos' against IWT, Tanzania created the National Taskforce Anti-Poaching (NTAP). Established in 2017, the NTAP was set up 'to achieve highly coordinated and intelligence-led joint anti-poaching activities', with standard operating procedures to guide its functioning approved the same year (MNRT , 2017[92]).

The NTAP brings together members of the Wildlife and Forest Crimes Taskforce and the National and Transnational Serious Crimes Investigation Unit's anti-poaching section. It comprises seconded officers from a range of agencies – from the country's wildlife and forestry agencies to the Tanzania Police Force, Tanzania People's Defence Force, Tanzania Intelligence and Security Service, Tanzania Prisons Service, Tanzania Immigration Service and, importantly, the PCCB (GA-07, 2017[44]).

The NTAP was cited repeatedly as an example of the benefits of multi-agency working from an anti-corruption perspective. According to one well-placed respondent, 'the key [of the NTAP] is to create a multi-agency structure where it is everyone's job to respond. This leaves little space for individual agencies to pass off an issue as 'not my problem' (GA-07, 2017[44])

A similar principle underlies the creation of joint units at key international export hubs, which can easily fall prey to corrupt actors working without inter-agency oversight. As such, as part of its Container Control Programme, UNODC has pursued the establishment of Joint Port Control Units across the region (UNODC, 2016[150]). This initiative seeks similarly to mitigate corruption risks through close inter-agency partnerships (Jayanathan, 2016[151]). These units exist in Kenya, Tanzania and Uganda – bringing together wildlife agencies, police, customs and ports authorities, among others. As noted by one respondent, 'from an anti-corruption perspective, it is crucial that such units exist and that representatives of each agency sit together in a single office. The accountability and transparency benefits that these structures brings could not be achieved in silos' (IO-01, 2017[61]) .

Such in-built accountability can be achieved in other ways, too. Respondents from several NGOs spoke in favour of strategic public–private partnerships to achieve accountability outcomes. (NG-06, 2017[58]) (NG-12, 2017[91]) (NG-14, 2017[108]) (NG-21, 2017[59]). These involve joint operating models on the ground and can take place at a range of levels – from anti-poaching to anti-trafficking activities. In particular, a number of respondents focused on the positive impacts of such partnerships in protected area management – where lack of oversight can enhance key corruption risks. (NG-06, 2017[58]) (NG-14, 2017[108]). Where NGOs or donors provide financial support, accountability can be enhanced through the incorporation of thorough checks and balances into partnership agreements (NG-12, 2017[91]) (NG-14, 2017[108]).

On this point, one respondent noted that 'at park level, a big advantage of public–private partnerships is that they reduce opportunities for corruption. The presence of another partner – whether private sector or NGO – reduces the ability of outsiders to interfere undetected. A wildlife management authority patrol unit alone may be easily intimidated or influenced. Where other actors are embedded, this becomes more challenging' (NG-06, 2017[58]).

At the same time, public-private structures creates joint interests as well as joint-accountability. This benefit can be achieved through MoUs between private-sector actors or NGOs and government agencies – whether wildlife management authorities or prosecution services, or other agencies. (NG-17, 2017[105]) (NG-18, 2017[38]) (NG-21, 2017[59]). According to one NGO, 'public–private partnerships increase accountability, making it more difficult for actors within a particular government agency to hide or bury cases' (NG-06, 2017[58]). Here, through officially agreed support to operations, external actors can increase accountability within the system. The existence of close public–private partnerships make scrutiny in line with checks and balances easier to achieve.

5.5. Addressing Corruption Risks: Accountability Mechanisms at Judicial Level

In all focus countries, respondents with prosecutorial expertise noted that anti-corruption efforts within the courts required more attention, further policy prescriptions and more concerted action. Numerous respondents observed the lack of anti-corruption targeting at this level – particularly in relation to IWT. As noted by Jayanathan in a 2016 analysis of criminal justice interventions, across African range states 'training and sensitisation of prosecutors and judges rarely … tackles the issue of corruption within the context of a criminal trial' (Jayanathan, 2016[151]). However, respondents highlighted the potential of several approaches to address these gaps.

In particular, respondents pointed to the value of developing IWT-focused Standard Operating Procedures (SOPs) for prosecutors. By clearly laying out the procedures prosecutors are to follow on IWT cases, respondents note the ability of such systems to professionalise IWT investigations and prosecutions (GA-09, 2017[71]) (GA-22, 2017[93]) (NG-04, 2017[97]) (NG-12, 2017[91]) (NG-13, 2017[73]) (NG-22, 2017[54]) (IO-02, 2017[42]). Importantly, they observe, through standardisation, SOPs can enhance transparency, allowing clearer identification of 'blockages' in the system (GA-09, 2017[71]) (NG-17, 2017[105]). SOPs can act as a check-list to be followed in order prevent nuances and recourse to explanations such as ignorance or lack of competence to 'mask' knowing corruption – a convenient 'grey area' referenced frequently by respondents (NG-21, 2017[59]) (NG-22, 2017[54]) (FD-04, 2017[122]) (FD-05, 2017[68]).

To date, prosecutors have adopted SOPs in Kenya, Tanzania and Uganda. These SOPs are often the result of a collaborative effort between government agencies, donor governments, international organisations and NGOs.[2] Most recently, SOPs were launched in Tanzania, coming into effect in January 2018. A total of 17 workshops were held on the new procedures, with over 450 prosecutors trained nationwide (MNRT , 2017[92]). From January 2018, the Director of Public Prosecutions in Tanzania has made use of the new SOPs mandatory, threatening punitive sanctions for anyone failing to comply (GA-09, 2017[71]) (NG-12, 2017[91]) (NG-13, 2017[73]).

In Kenya, further measures have been taken with similar transparency aims. At the same time, the recent launch of a pilot for 'active case management' to guide the conduct of IWT cases has aimed to reduce case backlog in the system. Rolled out in selected Kenyan courts, the pilot is a judge-driven process to meet the requirements of an effective trial. Involving a set of criminal procedures rules, active case management has positive anti-corruption benefits – by forcing all parties to play their prescribed roles (NG-02, 2017[96]) (NG-04, 2017[97]) (NG-08, 2017[107]). One important aspect of these case management procedures is the mandatory requirement for pre-trial conferences. Such conferences are intended to narrow down the issues under dispute, avoid unexpected delays, obstacles and lengthy adjournments that often plague due process. As such, respondents noted, they can play a positive role in avoiding case drift, and mitigating the corruption risks this entails (NG-02, 2017[96]) (NG-04, 2017[97]) (NG-13, 2017[73]) (NG-08, 2017[107]).

At the same time, the development of guidelines that set the bandwidth for sentencing around specific offences was cited as an important measure. The benefit of such policies was held to lie in the limitations they imply for magistrates' individual discretion in issuing sentences. In Kenya, a policy around these issues has been developed; in Uganda bandwidth guidance is set to be validated in 2018. In numerous other locations, however, action to develop these measures remains to be taken.

Alongside these actions, numerous respondents highlighted the value of raising awareness of IWT among prosecutors and magistrates (NG-13, 2017[73]) (NG-18, 2017[38]) (IE-03, 2017[124]). In some cases, magistrates have been taken on visits to reserves to experience the first-hand impact of IWT – and the corruption enabling it – in their own countries (GA-06, 2017[103]) (GA-09, 2017[71]) (NG-18, 2017[38]) (IO-02, 2017[42]) (IE-03, 2017[124]). As noted by TRAFFIC in a 2016 article, 'Currently there is little coverage of wildlife-related crimes and associated legislation in national law schools [in Tanzania] (TRAFFIC, 2016[152]). The overwhelming majority of the Tanzanian judiciary who responded to a TRAFFIC questionnaire said they had not received any relevant training'. In many cases, respondents cited the need for such sensitisation to make the target audience *feel* – not just know of – the harms caused by IWT. To do so, a multi-pronged approach is required, using elements that raise awareness such to emphasise the human – as well as environmental – costs of IWT.

Many such awareness-raising activities have already proven effective. However, many remain at pilot stage, and restricted to particular geographies (GA-06, 2017[103]) (GA-09, 2017[71]) (NG-13, 2017[73]) (NG-18, 2017[38]) (IO-02, 2017[42]) (IE-03, 2017[124]). For example, training targeting the judiciary has not occurred on a sufficiently comprehensive scale, with many continuing to hand out minimal sentences. In Zambia, most notably, previous initiatives have been limited in scale and geographical scope. As noted by Jayanathan, NGOs in the country have highlighted 'the need for more training and sensitisation of the judiciary on crimes involving endangered species', observing 'a particular and urgent need to address bushmeat-related offending'. (Jayanathan, 2016[151]). Additional funding and support is required to scale up existing initiatives and expand them to all affected locations.

5.6. Beyond Corruption Risks: The Need for Proactive Investigation

In addition to preventative measures to address corruption, the pro-active investigation of corruption-related offences is a crucial part of broader efforts to address IWT. As noted by one respondent, 'investigators typically focus exclusively on one line of enquiry – the trafficker himself; the predicate crime itself' (GA-02, 2017[83]). According to numerous respondents from government, NGOs and international organisations, law enforcement agencies tend to prioritise seizures and arrests as indicators of performance. Performance indicators are rarely related to the investigation of additional networks of corrupt facilitators further up the trafficking chain. However, respondents highlighted the value of conducting investigations into the predicate and ancillary offences. These could include investigations around the acceptance of bribes, tracing proceeds of crime and abuse of power. (GA-05, 2017[43]) (GA-02, 2017[83]) (NG-03, 2017[62]) (NG-05, 2017[110]) (NG-12, 2017[91]) (NG-13, 2017[73]) (NG-18, 2017[38]) (IE-03, 2017[124]) (IO-01, 2017[61]).

Numerous respondents noted that systematic parallel investigations into corruption related offences should be triggered after all seizures and arrests for IWT offences. Notably, trafficking cases should investigate the earlier transactions back to specific corrupt individuals earlier in the trade chain. Respondents acknowledged the difficulties in this work, which relate not least to obtaining hard evidence given the time that has often elapsed since the associated corrupt act was committed. (GA-05, 2017[43]) (GA-07, 2017[44]) (NG-01, 2017[72]) (NG-18, 2017[38]). There has also been a very limited focus on exploring additional charges given gaps in budget and capacity. However, a number of respondents highlighted the value of this work, particularly in conducting asset seizures and financial investigations to work towards a "follow the money" approach to IWT (GA-06, 2017[103]) (GA-07, 2017[44]) (GA-14, 2017[106]) (GA-21, 2017[74]) (NG-07, 2017[112]) (NG-12, 2017[91]) (NG-18, 2017[38]) (IO-02, 2017[42]) (IE-03, 2017[124]).

Indeed, in all focus countries, research by the Eastern and Southern African Anti-Money Laundering Group and Royal United Services Institute has shown the use of financial tools in IWT investigations and prosecutions to be limited. As concluded similarly by UNODC, 'To date, there have been very few attempts to "follow the money trail" by freezing and ultimately confiscating the proceeds of wildlife and forest crime, and identifying and criminalizing those who fund wildlife and forest offences or profit from them'. A similar view was offered by respondents, many of whom lamented the absence of financial approaches to investigating and prosecuting IWT cases. This is reinforced by analyses of court records, where these have been conducted in the focus countries. In Kenya, for example, an analysis of cases monitored by WildlifeDirect's Eyes in the Courtroom project during 2014 and 2015, shows the use of financial investigation evidence to have been almost entirely absent.

This situation is held to create numerous missed opportunities in relation to efforts to track corrupt facilitators. As those benefiting from IWT, respondents noted that corrupt actors are most likely to be discovered through the financial transactions that link them to those perpetrating the crime itself. Many also noted that the value of financial investigation in identifying such actors in relation to other crime types is well established. As such, respondents noted the urgent need for such tools to be extended into the wildlife sector.

Of course, tracking the finance of low-level criminals can be challenging in cash economies such as those of the focus countries. However, those who enable IWT are known to use non-cash systems to receive corrupt payments. Notably, even in rural parts of cash-based economies in East and Southern Africa, the use of mobile money systems for small bribes was held to offer fruitful potential leads. At the higher levels, meanwhile, the larger sums involved make it likely that the formal financial system is used. In a 2015 article, EIA describes it as 'inconceivable' that the amounts of money involved at trafficking level can be moved in cash, rather than through the banking system (EIA, 2015[153]) . Even where corrupt officers do not reveal themselves through their financial transactions, meanwhile, spending habits and often newly more sophisticated lifestyles can be scrutinised as part of investigations (Keatinge and Haenlein, 2017[154]).

Respondents thus noted the need for training and other support on the use of financial tools for investigators and prosecutors. Equally important was held to be increasing contact – particularly through establishing formal MoUs – between wildlife management authorities and financial intelligence units. Some work is underway in this area, with specific guidance on anti-money laundering tools provided as part of UNODC's 2012 'Wildlife and Forest Crime Analytic Toolkit'. Yet a lack of capacity has been identified clearly across the focus countries in implementing the guidance contained in the toolkit. As such, recent training has been delivered in Kenya, Uganda and Tanzania by the Royal United Services Institute; and in Kenya and Tanzania by the World Bank (RUSI, 2016[155]) (World Bank, 2017[156]). However, ongoing support to the use of financial approaches is required on a long-term operational basis (GA-07, 2017[44]) (GA-14, 2017[106]) (GA-21, 2017[74]) (NG-07, 2017[112]) (NG-12, 2017[91]) (IO-02, 2017[42]) (IE-03, 2017[124]).

The pursuit of financial approaches to investigating and prosecuting IWT requires cooperation with the private sector. This also applies more broadly: as noted in the G20 High Level Principles, engaging the private sector is crucial 'to encourage the adoption of adequate internal controls, upstream traceability systems in line with international standards, and ethics and compliance measures for businesses … engaged in legal trade' (G20, 2017[15]). Government respondents also noted the value of cooperation with private sector institutions active along the IWT supply chain (GA-12, 2017[57]).

5.7. Public Awareness Raising and Civil-Society Engagement

Public awareness and engagement is another valuable tool in enhancing the public spotlight on IWT and holding corrupt officials to account. In many cases, however, respondents complained that significant parts of civil society in the focus countries dismissed IWT as 'just about animals' without regard for the broader consequences (GA-18, 2017[52]). Corruption, meanwhile, is often not widely stigmatised, particularly when occurring in the wildlife sector. As one respondent noted, some may argue that 'a corrupt, rich man may be respected more highly than an honest but poor one' (GA-01, 2017[82]).

The media can play an important role in determining public perceptions of IWT and related corruption offences. Respondents cited a pressing need to train journalists on tools to report on corruption linked to IWT cases. Examples of media engagement include coverage of arrests of public officials and subsequent court cases. Other examples can include complex forms of investigative journalism that contribute in-depth information to the community on the depth, breadth and real costs of corruption.

Media involvement can also contribute positively to enhancing deterrence and prevention by raising public awareness of key law enforcement successes – acting as a signal to traffickers and their corrupt associates that the risks associated with IWT are real. The NGO EAGLE pursues this goal through the publication of media articles on arrests and prosecutions at a rate of one per day in each country of operation. The stated aim here is that of 'building deterrence by raising public awareness of the increased enforcement of wildlife laws and the increase risks and penalties' involved.

At the same time, NGO and civil society monitoring and reporting on IWT cases while they are in court provides valuable anti-corruption benefits. Respondents noted that donors could usefully propose additional support for public courtroom monitoring projects. For example, training of court monitors could allow civil society to participate more actively in monitoring court processes, while maintaining well appraised of the code of ethics governing the conduct of court and reporting of live cases. To ensure this, country-specific training and guidance on the conduct of court monitoring and surveys should be made available and promoted.[3]

5.8. The Need for Improved Data

Finally, respondents cited the need for improved data on corruption as an enabler of IWT. Here, they point to the lack of a wide baseline of convictions for corruption and the failure to systematically record associated corruption in known IWT incidents. Respondents suggested that systematic data collection on types of corruption facilitating IWT, and greater transparency through electronic record keeping, could assist law enforcement and increase awareness of the scale of the problem. On this point, some respondents cited the need to address gaps in existing formats for reporting IWT. They did so noting, for example, the Illegal Trade Reporting Requirement promulgated at the CITES Standing Committee meeting in January 2016, which lacks a dedicated section on corruption in relation to stated 'reasons for seizure'.

Respondents noted that that reporting requirements for corruption serve important benefits. A structured reporting system can assist in triggering the parallel corruption-focused investigations called for above, by drawing attention to their relevance to each case. Second, the systematic recording of this data will expand, over time, the volume of information recorded on corruption linked to IWT. This will in turn allow more detailed analysis of the forms, manifestations and dynamics of corruption most commonly witnessed over time.

Such an expanded repository of data on the corruption fuelling IWT is urgently needed. As noted throughout this report, a comprehensive understanding of the dynamics involved is critical to the effective targeting of anti-corruption initiatives. Generating better data on the role of corruption in IWT is an endeavour on which our collective efforts must now focus.

References

EAGLE Network (2018), "Anti-Corruption", http://www.eagle-enforcement.org/anti-corruption/.

GA-04 (2017), "REPRESENTATIVE OF GOVERNMENT AGENCY 7: In person Interview, Friday 8 September, 2017".

GA-06 (2017), "REPRESENTATIVE OF GOVERNMENT AGENCY 9: In person interview, Thursday 14 December 2017".

GA-08 (2017), "REPRESENTATIVES OF GOVERNMENT AGENCY 12, 13: In person interview, Friday 15 December 2017".

GA-11 (2017), "REPRESENTATIVES OF GOVERNMENT AGENCY 17, 18, 19: In person interview, Tuesday 5 September 2017".

GA-13 (2017), "REPRESENTATIVE OF GOVERNMENT AGENCY 22: In person interview, Tuesday 5 September,".

GA-14 (2017), "REPRESENTATIVE OF GOVERNMENT AGENCY 23: In person interview, Wednesday 6 September 2017".

GA-17-2017 (2017), "REPRESENTATIVE OF GOVERNMENT AGENCY 25: In person interview, Monday 11 December 2017".

GA-20 (2017), "REPRESENTATIVES OF GOVERNMENT AGENCY 31, 32: In person Interview, Tuesday 12 December 2017".

IO-02 (2017), "REPRESENTATIVE OF INTERNATIONAL ORGANISATION 3: In person interview, 15 December 2017".

Keatinge, T. and C. Haenlein (2017), *Follow the Money: Using Financial Investigation to Combat Wildlife Crime*, https://rusi.org/sites/default/files/201709_rusi_follow_the_money_haenlein.keatinge.pdf..

KFS (2010), "Kenya Forestry Service '"Walking the Talk": Corruption Perception Baseline Survey'", http://www.kenyaforestservice.org/documents/KFS%20Final%20Report%20Corruption.pdf.

KWS (2017), "Review of KWS Standing Orders and Disciplinary Code", http://www.kws.go.ke/content/review-kws-standing-orders-and-disciplinary-code.

KWS et. al. (2016), *Rapid Reference Guide for the Investigation and Prosecution of Wildlife Related Offences Including Standard Operating Procedures and Sample Charges*, https://wildlifedirect.org/wp-content/uploads/2017/03/R.

NG-05 (2017), "REPRESENTATIVE OF NGO 5: In person interview, Saturday 9 September, 2017".

NG-08 (2017), "REPRESENTATIVE OF NGO 33: In person interview, Monday 11 September, 2017".

NG-14 (2017), "REPRESENTATIVES OF NGO 13, 14: In person interview, Thursday 14 December 2017".

NG-16 (2017), "REPRESENTATIVES OF NGO 17, 18: In person interview, Monday 4 September 2017".

NG-17 (2017), "REPRESENTATIVE OF NGO 19, 20: In person interview, Monday 4 September, 2017".

NG-19 (2017), "REPRESENTATIVE OF NGO 22: In person interview, Wednesday 6 September 2017".

RUSI (2016), *New Research Project Funded by UK Government to Track Funds from Illegal Wildlife Trade*, https://rusi.org/rusi-news/new-research-project-funded-uk-government-track-funds-illegal-wildlife-trade.

Space for Giants((n.d.)), *Court Surveys on the Handling of Wildlife Crime – A Guidance*.

Transparency International (2017), "Corruption Perceptions Index 2017", https://www.transparency.org/news/feature/corruption_perceptions_index_2017.

UNODC (2016), "Programme to enhance container security extends its global reach", https://www.unodc.org/unodc/en/frontpage/2016/March/programme-to-enhance-container-security-extends-its-global-reach.html.

World Bank (2017), *Global Wildlife Program*, http://www.worldbank.org/en/topic/environment/brief/global-wildlife-program.

Notes

[1] Although notable exceptions include the work of the Eco Activists for Governance and Law Enforcement (EAGLE) Network and UNODC's Global Programme for Combating Wildlife and Forest Crime.

[2] See for example, Kenya Wildlife Service Rapid Reference Guide for the Investigation and Prosecution of Wildlife Related Offences (KWS et. al., 2016[171])

[3] See, for example, Space for Giants, 'Court Surveys on the Handling of Wildlife Crime – A Guidance', no date, http://spaceforgiants.org/wp-content/uploads/2017/11/Court-survey-guidance-Final.pdf

6. Conclusion: Developing effective governance frameworks to stop IWT

This concluding chapter outlines the findings of this study, and provides a comprehensive set of detailed recommendations to governments, the broader donor community and other non-governmental actors on how to better address corruption risks and counter IWT.

'A system to combat IWT is in place, but it is built around avoiding the big question – corruption. Corruption is not simply another aspect of IWT – it cannot be treated as an add-on. It is the air wildlife traffickers breathe' (NG-05, 2017[110]) .

Addressing corruption as an enabler of IWT has not been treated as a priority in source and transit countries to date. International donors have not focused on countering corruption linked to IWT; as such, this is too often treated simply as an unavoidable operating reality. However, the role of corruption as an enabler of IWT in the focus countries has limited the effectiveness of the internationally agreed system to counter IWT. As this report has shown, IWT-related corruption is multi-faceted; it is found across numerous agencies, sectors, individuals and activities at various levels of public administration. To effectively combat illegal wildlife trade, donors will have to place the corruption that enables it at the front and centre of their policies and programmes.

In considering the most effective means to disrupt corruption linked to IWT in source and transit countries, it is useful to review how corruption in this sphere differs from that in other sectors. Of significance here is the traditionally low profile accorded to IWT in the eyes of publics and governments alike. As such, even as IWT has grown into one of the largest forms of transnational organised crime worldwide, institutional frameworks to combat it have remained weak and disorganised. The burden is largely carried by under-resourced wildlife management authorities unaccustomed to addressing serious transnational crime. As a result, the risks facing both wildlife traffickers and, importantly, corrupt facilitators remain low. All too often, the prospect of interception or punishment remains minimal.

An additional unique factor characterising corruption linked to IWT concerns the complex legal status of many wildlife products. The result is the existence of parallel markets – in which legal and illegal products can mix freely. The unclear status of many species – combined with the underdeveloped status of global permitting systems – creates abundant opportunities for corrupt actors to facilitate illegal trade. The lack of transparency is exacerbated by the absence of electronic recordkeeping or a universal permit database.

Further unique features of corruption linked to IWT in source and transit countries revolve around the remote rural locations involved and the autonomy of officers in those locations. The distance of these officers from management structures – alongside poor and irregular pay – creates ample risks across affected countries. At the same time, vulnerabilities lie in the frequent institutional handovers often seen in IWT cases. Here, risks lie at the multiple seams between areas of responsibility. Notably, the lack of overarching institutional jurisdiction means that gaps in communication, prioritisation and responsibility are easily exploited.

These unique features mean that a small amount of corrupt conducts can have a very significant impact. Together, these factors make it all too easy for those who want to corrupt to 'influence' those charged with wildlife protection. The result is perhaps more damaging than that seen in other sectors – owing to the finite status of wildlife resources. Unlike drugs, arms and numerous other commodities trafficked across the globe, when wildlife has run out, it cannot easily be replaced.

This consideration places considerable importance not only on investigating and effectively prosecuting corruption as an enabler of IWT. In addition, it underlines the importance, in this case, of proactive corruption prevention. This study puts forward recommendations in all three areas: corruption prevention and awareness; investigation;

and prosecution and sentencing. These apply specifically to corruption enabling IWT and are as follows.

6.1. Detailed Recommendations

The below recommendations have been developed within the scope of the current analysis. These detailed recommendations reflect the positions of experts and the research of the OECD and a number of best practises identified throughout the interviews conducted. The recommendations are aimed at governments and relevant authorities in affected countries, as well as at donor countries and international organisations specializing in assistance and capacity building. Some of these recommendations may be considered beyond a regional context for their wider geographical and policy relevance to address the IWT as a global threat.

6.1.1. Recommendations to Governments

- Support multi-agency anti-poaching and anti-trafficking structures that incorporate wildlife management authorities and anti-corruption authorities, alongside police forces and other security agencies.
- Strengthen prevention by developing and enforcing codes of conduct for public officials. Ensure that all government agencies treat internal corruption related to IWT unambiguously as a criminal offence. Where corruption is uncovered, all agencies should be prepared to refer the officer in question to the anti-corruption authority.
- Acknowledge the importance of global anti-corruption efforts in combatting IWT. Engage relevant international and regional conventions on anti-corruption and associated frameworks. Actions can include:
    - Making use of existing OECD instruments on integrity and corruption, such as the 2017 OECD Council Recommendation on Public Integrity and others.
    - Making use of the UN Convention against Corruption (UNCAC) to tackle IWT.
    - Applying the recommendations of the Financial Action Task Force (FATF) on anti-money laundering with respect to corrupt actors and the application of money laundering charges to all serious offences.
- Use financial investigation tools as part of a 'follow the money' approach. Concerted efforts must be made to ensure that those charged with tackling IWT have the necessary skills to conduct financial investigations. Such tools can be particularly powerful in ensuring that the prosecutorial net includes not just the trafficker in question, but ensnares corrupt actors who have benefitted financially along the way.
- Tackle the high risk of corruption associated with stockpiles by adopting systems to enhance accounting and transparency. Designated authorities should consolidate and control access to storerooms housing stockpiles, and develop security and traceability measures such as surveillance technology, joint entry requirements and electronic record keeping.
- Ensure systematic collection of corruption data (arrests, prosecutions, convictions) to capture risk factors and allow the development of more detailed typologies[1].

Wildlife Management Authorities

- Support the reform and expansion of existing integrity and anti-corruption policies within wildlife management authorities.
  - Develop effective HR management policies. Ensure a fair and open recruitment process and integrate integrity profiles into hiring practises. Use tools such as background checks for recruitment of new individuals and carry out periodical integrity reviews of employees moving into high-risk positions or senior leadership roles.
  - At the beginning and throughout the careers of public officials, offer induction and on-the-job training of public officials for integrity, and codes of conduct. Maintain culture of openness, and provide clear rules for procedures for reporting and following up with suspected cases of corrupt behaviour.
  - Develop a culture of leadership through integrity. Support managers in their roles as ethical leaders within headquarters as well as in the field. Use integrity assessments and records of good conduct as part of the performance measurement of officers for promotion or appointments, particularly in the more remote field locations.
- Liaise directly with anti-corruption authorities to exchange information and knowledge on corruption risks related to IWT.
- Undertake assessments of local-level incentive structures. At the park level, develop policies with performance and integrity-based rewards in mind. For example, consider mechanisms to reward rangers, scouts and members of the public for reporting and assisting in successful anti-poaching and -trafficking investigations.
- Employ technology and innovative solutions to make specific tasks more resilient against corruption. Support automation of key wildlife management processes as part of broader anti-corruption interventions and remove human discretion where possible. The use of technology to assist in mitigating corruption risks can include the automation of payment transactions and the tracking of ranger patrol movements while on active duty.
- Support strategic cooperation with private and other non-governmental actors to achieve key accountability and transparency outcomes. Such cooperation can be effective at the level of protected-area management, where lack of oversight can hamper visibility. Public-private partnerships can also be effective at central level, where NGOs maintain MoUs to provide strategic input and investigate or prosecute on behalf of wildlife management authorities and other government agencies.
- Consult anti-corruption authorities and international best practises for witness and whistle-blower protection. In particular, wildlife management and other authorities should increase the level and type of protection offered to witnesses and whistle-blowers, in line with broader OECD guidelines[2].

Customs, Police and Relevant Investigatory Agencies

- Study and thoroughly investigate incidents at border points and in airports to identify gaps and abnormalities that suggest corrupt practises at play. Particular attention should be paid to exemptions from inspection of VIP areas and cargo processing sections at airports.

- Where possible, employ technological solutions to make human interference more difficult, such as the use of scanning technology and K-9 tools at inspection points.
- Given the prevalence of corruption as an enabler of IWT, agencies should develop and complete an investigatory checklist of corruption indicators to guide this process. Investigators must place emphasis on 'tracing back' corrupt facilitation across earlier stages of the supply chain by exploring prior actions and facilitating measures that are likely to have enabled goods to arrive at the point of seizure untouched.
- Liaise with anti-corruption authorities to exchange corruption related information to IWT.
- Liaise with financial intelligence units and ensure that, in line with Financial Action Task Force Recommendation 30, parallel financial investigations are conducted following all major incidents. Liaise at the international level with partner countries as part of these investigations.
- Support regional and international cooperation. At a regional level, cross-border taskforces have the potential to facilitate operations and information sharing on IWT and associated corruption on a rapid basis.
- Countries should employ information sharing treaties (such as mechanisms for asset recovery, customs mutual assistance agreements, and, mutual legal assistance agreements,) to compare and interrogate discrepancies, trace arrests, and verify suspicious documentation across borders. Such processes can help to encourage customs officials at point of import to challenge corrupt facilitation further down the chain.

Public Prosecutors and Magistrates

- Use available ancillary legislation: where official collusion is detected, public officers engaged in actions to enable IWT should be tried under anti-corruption or economic-crime legislation. This often offers stronger penalties and wider-reaching asset-forfeiture provisions than wildlife acts.
- Freeze, seize and confiscate assets. This can offer a powerful deterrent beyond the small fines and short custodial sentences often seen to date, and can allow the reinvestment of seized assets into measures to disrupt both IWT and associated corruption.
- Employ active case management procedures. Transparency aims should be pursued at judicial level through a magistrate-driven process to actively manage the requirements of trial. Such procedures can ensure that all parties play their prescribed roles, reducing case backlog in the system. The use of pre-trial conferences can narrow down the issues under dispute and anticipate potential obstacles.
- Develop and enforce IWT-focused standard operating procedures (SOPs) to guide wildlife-focused prosecutions. Such SOPs serve to standardise and unambiguously lay out the procedures that prosecutors must follow on IWT cases. This can assist with strengthening control over evidence and court exhibits, among other issues.
- Develop sentencing guidelines for specific IWT and corruption offences, thus setting an acceptable bandwidth and appropriate upper and lower sanctions for judicial decisions. The anti-corruption benefit of such policies lies in the

limitations they imply for magistrates' discretion in issuing sentences. This can apply to both IWT offences and those linked to associated corruption.

- Support efforts to digitise case records to facilitate the extraction and monitoring over time of relevant patterns and trends. This can be useful for case file analysis and performance reporting and inform the design of accountability measures.

6.1.2. Donors and Development Agencies

- Take proactive steps to address corruption head on in the design of donor funded projects. Prioritise and target structural vulnerabilities (i.e. in reporting, codes of conduct, oversight) in wildlife-focused law enforcement and criminal justice structures.
- Promote anti-corruption efforts as an essential component of international conferences and actions on IWT. Prioritise anti-corruption efforts in fora such as CITES, G7, or G20, by including wildlife and environmental crime in the development of anti-corruption principles and practises.
- Prior to approving a donor-funded project, conduct comprehensive corruption risk assessments, taking into account specific risks, as well as transparency and accountability mechanisms that will be implemented such that spending does not inadvertently facilitate corruption in affected locations. This may involve the development of corruption risk-assessments or checklists.[3]
- Support regional and international law enforcement cooperation around anti-corruption cases. Leverage Mutual Legal Assistance agreements and other treaties to address the multinational nature of this crime, in recognition of the role of foreign actors who act with impunity in the financing of corruption and IWT.
- Train relevant staff of anti-corruption authorities on issues specific to IWT to enhance officers' knowledge and awareness. Enhance expertise through joint international workshops, learning exchanges and working groups to develop better processes and policies that target IWT-related corruption offences.
- Provide IWT-focused training for prosecutors and magistrates. Training and sensitisation programmes targeting prosecutors and magistrates should focus on the causes and costs of IWT and highlight the economic, human and ecological damage caused by the corruption that enables it.
- Where possible, provide expert guidance and assistance to magistrates and prosecutors to build capacities to process corruption cases. Assist in the development of SOPs and active case management procedures for prosecutors working on IWT and corruption cases.
- Facilitate media engagement in the court process. To enhance accountability mechanisms, 'eyes in the courtroom' programmes should be resourced and scaled up nationwide in focus countries. This must be done while keeping well appraised of the code of ethics governing the conduct of court and reporting of live cases. As part of this, country-specific training and guidance on the conduct of court monitoring and surveys should be made available and promoted.[4]
- Support initiatives that collect and harmonise additional sources of data on corruption cases. Promote development of common reporting standards for corruption incidents.
- In global fora, support a CITES electronic permitting system. The efforts of the CITES Secretariat to move from a paper-based permitting system towards an

electronic one must be supported as a priority. Universal electronic permitting would enhance resilience to physical forgery and allow the development of a centralised database of CITES records, with the eventual goal of tracking and tracing certain products. This, in turn, could allow the automatic reconciliation of export and import records.

References

Allison, S. (2011), *Zambian President: Our Wildlife is Fair Game*, https://www.dailymaverick.co.za/article/2011-10-31-zambian-president-our-wildlife-is-fair-game/.

Bwire, J. (2017), *Uganda apologises to China over ivory smuggling scandal*, http://www.monitor.co.ug/News/National/Uganda-apologises-to-China-over-ivory-smuggling-scandal/688334-3967166-15f436y/index.html.

Daily News Tanzania (2017), *Police officers jailed 35 years on poaching charges*, https://www.dailynews.co.tz/index.php/home-news/53046-police-officers-jailed-35-years-on-poaching-charges.

Deutsche Welle (2017), *Rangers colluding with elephant poachers in Tanzania*, http://www.dw.com/en/rangers-colluding-with-elephant-poachers-in-tanzania/av-41837902.

FD-05 (2017), “REPRESENTATIVES OF FOREIGN DELEGATION 8, 9: Development Affairs Advisors, In Person Interview, Monday 11 December 2017”.

GA-10 (2017), “REPRESENTATIVE OF GOVERNMENT AGENCY 16: In person interview, Sunday 3 September 2017”.

GA-21 (2017), “REPRESENTATIVE OF GOVERNMENT AGENCY 33: In person interview, Tuesday 12 December, 2017”.

Great Elephant Census (2015), *Uganda’s Elephants Thriving According to Preliminary Census Results*, http://www.greatelephantcensus.com/blog/2015/6/2/ugandas-elephants-thriving.

Great Elephant Census (2016), “Zambia Census Results Announced: Luangwa and Kafue Stable, Lower Zambezi Declines and Sioma Ngwezi Declines Catastrophically”, http://www.greatelephantcensus.com/blog/2016/3/2/zambia-census-announced-luangwa-and-kafue-stable-lower-zambezi-and-sioma-ngwezi-see-decline.

IE-02-2017 (2017), “INDEPENDENT EXPERT 2: In person interview, Saturday 9 September 2017”.

IE-05 (2017), “INDEPENDENT EXPERT 5: In person interview, Monday 11 December 2017”.

IO-01 (2017), “REPRESENTATIVES OF INTERNATIONAL ORGANISATION 1, 2: In person Interview, Friday 8 September, 2017”.

Jamiyeto (2016), *Policemen Poachers Jailed 20 Years*, http://dailyevents310.blogspot.co.uk/2016/03/policemen-poachers-jailed-20yrs.html.

Kaaya, S. (2017), *Ivory Scam Claims - China Piles Pressure On Uganda*, http://allafrica.com/stories/201706050298.html.

Kahumbu, P. (2016), *Kenya Jails Ivory Kingpin for 20 Years*, https://www.theguardian.com/environment/africa-wild/2016/jul/23/kenya-jails-ivory-kinpin-for-20-years.

Koech, G. (2017), *'Elephant poaching declines in Kenya, focus turns to world markets'*, https://www.the-star.co.ke/news/2017/11/30/elephant-poaching-declines-in-kenya-focus-turns-to-world-markets_c1677846.

Lilongwe Wildlife Trust (2016), *Zambian Army Captain Imprisoned in Malawi for Wildlife Trafficking*, https://www.lilongwewildlife.org/2016/09/30/zambian-army-captain-imprisoned-malawi-wildlife-trafficking/.

Lusaka Times (2011), *670 "Wildlife" Prisoners Pardoned*, https://www.lusakatimes.com/2011/10/24/670-wildlife-prisoners-pardoned/.

Mafabi, D. (2017), *IGG probes Uganda Wildlife Authority*, http://www.monitor.co.ug/News/National/IGG-probes-Uganda-Wildlife-Authority/688334-3949978-mjwrabz/index.html.

Mafabi, D. (2017), *IGG probes Uganda Wildlife Authority*, http://www.monitor.co.ug/News/National/IGG-probes-Uganda-Wildlife-Authority/688334-3949978-mjwrabz/index.html.

Mathiesen, K. (2015), "Tanzania elephant population declined by 60% in five years, census reveals", *Guardian*, http://dx.doi.org/Tanzania elephant population declined by 60% in five years, census reveals'.

Namugerwa, M. (2017), *Museveni Directs IGG to Suspend UWA Boss Seguya Over Corruption, Smuggling, Mismanagement of Wildlife Body*.

Ndagire, B. (2017), *Uganda: Soldiers Fined Shs4 Million for Stealing Ivory*, http://allafrica.com/stories/201703010085.html.

NG-06 (2017), "REPRESENTATIVE OF NGO 6: In person interview, Saturday 9 September 2017".

NG-07 (2017), "REPRESENTATIVE OF NGO 7: In person interview, Monday 11 September 2017".

NG-22 (2017), "REPRESENTATIVE OF NGO 26: In person interview, Monday 11 December 2017".

Republic of Zambia (2015), "Report on the 2015 Aerial Survey in Zambia: Population Estimates of African Elephants (Loxodonta africana) in Zambia", *Nature*, Vol. 1, https://www.nature.org/ourinitiatives/regions/africa/zambia-great-elephant-census-report.pdf.

RI-01 (2017), "REPRESENTATIVE OF RESEARCH INSTITUTE 1: In person interview, Wednesday 13 December 2017".

Vaughan, A. (2016), *Kenya's new front in poaching battle: "the future is in the hands of our communities"*, https://www.theguardian.com/environment/2016/may/30/kenya-poaching-elephant-ivory-rhino-horn-future-communities.

Wasser et al. (2015), "Genetic Assignment of Large Seizures of Elephant Ivory Reveals Africa's Major Poaching Hotspots", *Science*.

Wolpert, S. (2015), *Which is most valuable: Gold, cocaine or rhino horn?*, http://newsroom.ucla.edu/releases/which-is-most-valuable-gold-cocaine-or-rhino-horn.

Notes

[1] As part of this, there is a need to develop new approaches to the registration IWT data, as part of broader processes for recording seizures and arrests by harmonising data elements such as weight, type, etc. Existing reporting requirements – such as those promulgated at the CITES Standing Committee meeting in January 2016 – must be augmented such that they require the recording corruption or other proximate terms (such as those recorded in the open-source corruption media mapping undertaken in this report).

[2] As part of this, they should provide officers with options to refer accusations of corruption directly to anti-corruption authorities, with dedicated training on the procedures for doing so, and allow for the effective protection of witnesses testifying in cases linked to corruption and IWT in accordance with international guidance, such as the OECD Whistle-blower Protection Guidelines.

[3] During the design of any counter-IWT intervention, dedicated corruption risk-assessments should be conducted with appropriate checks and balances incorporated. These assessments – and the resulting risk-management systems developed – must be flexible, recognising the diversity and complexity of corruption risks outlined in this report, and their propensity to evolve over the life of a programme.

4 See, for example, Space for Giants, 'Court Surveys on the Handling of Wildlife Crime – A Guidance' (Space for Giants,(n.d.)[172])

ORGANISATION FOR ECONOMIC CO-OPERATION AND DEVELOPMENT

The OECD is a unique forum where governments work together to address the economic, social and environmental challenges of globalisation. The OECD is also at the forefront of efforts to understand and to help governments respond to new developments and concerns, such as corporate governance, the information economy and the challenges of an ageing population. The Organisation provides a setting where governments can compare policy experiences, seek answers to common problems, identify good practice and work to co-ordinate domestic and international policies.

The OECD member countries are: Australia, Austria, Belgium, Canada, Chile, the Czech Republic, Denmark, Estonia, Finland, France, Germany, Greece, Hungary, Iceland, Ireland, Israel, Italy, Japan, Korea, Latvia, Lithuania, Luxembourg, Mexico, the Netherlands, New Zealand, Norway, Poland, Portugal, the Slovak Republic, Slovenia, Spain, Sweden, Switzerland, Turkey, the United Kingdom and the United States. The European Union takes part in the work of the OECD.

OECD Publishing disseminates widely the results of the Organisation's statistics gathering and research on economic, social and environmental issues, as well as the conventions, guidelines and standards agreed by its members.

OECD PUBLISHING, 2, rue André-Pascal, 75775 PARIS CEDEX 16
(42 2018 42 1 P) ISBN 978-92-64-30649-3 – 2018

www.ingramcontent.com/pod-product-compliance
Lightning Source LLC
LaVergne TN
LVHW081413110826
845149LV00010B/1734

9789264306493